THE
FIRE
WITHIN

B.J. Hansen

ACCENT BOOKS
Denver, Colorado

Kevin about it, but he just said Adam had some personal problems he was trying to deal with. She was glad her boss was a Christian, and it touched Kelly to know Kevin was so concerned about Adam. But then, there were a lot of things about Kevin that Kelly liked.

He reminded Kelly of her younger brother back home. It was easy to like him. She wasn't sure, but she thought Maggie was rather fond of Kevin too; she seemed to blossom in his presence. Mags had admitted as much on one occasion when she'd conceded that she never felt so alive as she did when in Kevin's company.

Kelly knew the feeling a little too well. "Enough of that!" she scolded herself.

As she hurried into the building, Kelly could hear the presses gearing up in the back room, but the front offices were deserted. She threw off her parka and went directly to the dark room. Forty-five minutes later, Kelly emerged with a handful of proof sheets. Jason was at his computer terminal finishing up the arson story.

Jason Roberts was a mystery to Kelly. He rarely spoke to anyone unless it was about business. The only exception Kelly noticed was that once in a while she saw him consulting with Maggie in confidential tones. But Mags had never volunteered any information, and Kelly had been reluctant to pry. To everyone else, he remained aloof, alone and guarded. That's why his next words surprised her so.

"Kelly, you want to grab a bite to eat? I think we deserve a break after this last assignment. Besides, I need to ask you something about this case."

She turned to him, sure the surprise she felt showed in her face.

"I–I can't. I mean, I've got quite a lot of work to finish up, here." She apologized. "But I'd be happy to discuss the case with you right now, if you like."

"Tell you what," Jason countered. "How about if I go get us

14

a couple of hamburgers and bring them back here? That ought to give you enough time to finish up whatever you have to do."

"Sounds good. But only if you let me pay my fair share." Kelly reached for her shoulder bag, waving away his protest. She spent a minute or two sifting through the clutter, searching for her wallet.

Her brothers used to tease her unmercifully about the amount of miscellany her purse could hold and she always seemed to have it crammed just as full as she could get it.

"There!" she said triumphantly as she handed him a fistful of dollar bills and change. "Make mine a quarter pounder, fries, and a chocolate shake."

Jason took the money and got up to put on his overcoat. "Tell Adam the story's all set. All he has to do is punch it up when he's ready for it."

"He's still here?" Kelly asked. "I thought he'd be long gone by now."

"Not when he's working on the arson story."

"I don't understand..."

"Let's just say he's got a personal interest in this."

Kelly wondered at his inference as she watched him leave. Maybe she could get him to tell her more later.

Kelly was quickly immersed in her work, trying unsuccessfully to pick out a front page photo. She was so absorbed that she wasn't aware anyone was behind her until she felt a hand on her shoulder. The bolt that shot through her at his touch made her gasp as she turned to meet the penetrating eyes of Adam Wentworth.

3

Kelly wished the electricity pulsing through her body could be explained away by the suddenness of the encounter. But, captivated by those mesmerizing gray eyes, she knew there was more to her pounding heart than just being startled.

Adam's good looks always seemed to take her by surprise. She knew he couldn't be more than a few inches taller than she was, but his broad chest and powerful arms and shoulders seemed to amplify his presence in the room. Perhaps it was the superbly developed physique that made him appear taller than he actually was.

Maggie had mentioned once that Adam had been a championship wrestler in college and had won several honors for his skills in the martial arts during his stint in the Marines. It was obvious he continued to work out on a regular basis.

Kelly tried to regain her composure, but, taken totally off guard and being so near him, she could scarcely breathe.

She felt a little bit trapped under his gaze and tried to break away from him by shifting her own eyes to the amused curve of his full lower lip and the slight crinkle that settled in his right cheek. Just beneath it lay the faintest reminder of a finely stitched scar that ran almost the entire length of his jaw. Kelly

"Evidence? What evidence!" Jason's face lit up like a radar unit. "Are you saying they've got something concrete to go on?"

"Well, not really. I mean, it's only speculation, but I did happen to hear a couple of the firemen mention they might have discovered something behind the site of this last fire. But really, Jason, it's just something I overheard. There may be nothing to it at all!"

"I thought I saw you talking to a couple of them this afternoon. So? What did they find? Where was this supposed to have been? Are they sending the evidence to the state crime lab?"

The barrage of questions were volleyed at her. Kelly put her hand up in an effort to stop the torrent.

"Jason...Jason. Really! I don't have any answers for you. All I know is that one of the firemen said that they *might*, and I stress the word *might*, have found something at the back of the building. I'm sure they haven't had a chance to examine it because of the mess from the fire and the fact that it was getting so dark. They probably can't even take a good look at it until early tomorrow. So please, enough already!"

"Sorry, Kelly. It's just my nature, I guess. And this story is very important to me." Jason gave a short laugh. "But then, you've probably already figured that out. Sorry for coming on so strong."

Jason dropped the subject for a while as the conversation drifted into small talk, but he seemed preoccupied. Kelly could almost see the wheels turning in his head as he plotted his next move.

Kelly didn't envy George McClanahan. After their conversation earlier that day, she knew he would be the most likely target for Jason's next interview.

But something was bothering her. Finally, she gave in to her curiosity and plied Jason with her own questions.

"Jason," she began, "remember, before you left? You said

something about Adam's interest in this case. Well, I was wondering…why does he seem so intense when it comes to this story?"

"It isn't just *this* story," Jason replied. "He's obsessed with arson fires in general."

Kelly's eyebrows shot up in inquisitive arcs.

"It all started about this time last year when Adam's house burned to the ground. He lost everything—including his wife."

Kelly drew a quick breath.

"The fire department said it looked like some oily rags caught fire in the garage. Said it could have been the fault of an old electric heater they'd stored there, but Adam was convinced it was no accident. He thought it was arson. Apparently there had been several suspicious fires in the area at the time, but no one was able to prove anything one way or the other."

"You say, apparently. Weren't you around then?"

"Oh, yes, I was here, but they hadn't yet discovered my considerable journalistic talent at the time. They had me writing obits and covering garden shows."

Even though Jason laughed as he spoke the words, Kelly detected a hint of resentment in his voice.

"Anyway, Adam made a big deal of the whole thing, wrote a couple of editorials that weren't exactly complimentary to our local fire department, and demanded the removal of the fire chief—who just happened to be Mr. George McClanahan.

"Fortunately for him, he had some pull with City Hall and got himself moved over to the fire investigation team at the police department. Now you can see why it's so hard for me to get any information out of him. The whole thing was a big mess and, ironically, they never were able to prove whether it was arson or not.

"Frankly, I thought Adam would have been better off if he would have dropped his vendetta against McClanahan. I told Adam as much, but, like I said, he was obsessed with the whole thing.

"I did everything possible to try to help. Even went and did a little digging on my own. You'd think he would have been grateful. After all, it was that particular series that won me my Tri-County News Award. But instead, he turns on me. Says I'm out of line. That it wasn't my assignment and that I'd better watch out or I'd be writing obits the rest of my life."

Kelly felt the air grow thick with Jason's bitterness.

"Perhaps you shouldn't be too hard on him, Jason." Kelly tried to shift the direction of the conversation. "Adam must have been terribly distraught over his loss. I know how devastating that can be. I lost someone myself not too long ago…my father. We were very close, and it was a real shock for me. It must have been the same for Adam, too. I can't imagine he would turn on you like that unless he was just so overcome with grief that he wasn't thinking clearly."

Jason shrugged off her explanation. "If that was the case, he should have taken a leave of absence like the corporation recommended instead of taking it out on everyone else."

In the awkward silence that followed, Kelly searched frantically for some other topic to introduce, but deliverance came from an unexpected source.

"Well, isn't this cozy!" Whitney's voice dripped with sarcasm from the doorway near Maggie's desk.

It seemed as if she had been through some sort of metamorphosis since that afternoon. Instead of the harsh-looking braided knot she had been wearing earlier, her ebony mane now flowed softly around her face. Shades of pastel eye shadow and dark eye liner set off her eyes.

She wore an alluring black satin jumpsuit accentuated with strategically placed rhinestones along the deep "V" neckline. An emerald choker caressed her throat and emerald rings sparkled on her fingers. A black chinchilla cape was flung carelessly across her arms and shoulders. She obviously had spent a great deal of time and energy to create this captivating effect, and Kelly wondered who was going to get

23

the full benefit of the outfit.

"If it isn't Peter Perfect and Paula Pious," Whitney purred. "Settling for second best, huh, Jason? Well, I must say, you make an ideal couple. In this corner—Jason Roberts, Mr. Know-It-All, constantly searching for ways to feed his enormous ego. And in this corner—Kelly Jordan, Patron Saint of the Polaroid Print."

"I don't remember inviting any alley cats to this party, do you, Kelly?" Jason sneered. "Perhaps we should contact the local pound and let them know one of their inmates escaped."

"Just because you got stuck with a dog like Kelly, doesn't mean you have to get nasty," Whitney spat back.

"Why don't you go find someone else to sharpen your claws on!" Jason bristled. "Or is that the problem? I dumped you and Adam won't have anything to do with you, so now you can't find a pack to run with tonight."

"For your information, my date's waiting for me right now." Whitney returned. "I just stopped to get something."

She moved toward them, pausing at her desk briefly to pick up an object. As she slid it inside her purse, she turned toward Jason.

"The fact that I have a new boyfriend is what's really bugging you, isn't it, Jason?" Whitney placed herself directly in his line of sight. "You just can't stand the fact you were easily replaced. Only this time, I've found a real man! Not some sick, egotistical wimp like you!"

Jason jumped to his feet and clenched Whitney's arm in a steely grip. For a brief instant Kelly was terrified that Jason might actually strike Whitney, but almost as quickly, he released her.

"You're not worth it, my dear." He settled back in the chair and seemed to tune her out completely.

"Jason, I think it's time I left." Kelly reached for her shoulder bag.

"Don't let this she-devil get to you," Jason implored. "She

isn't worth getting upset over."

"No, really. It's been a long day and I am very tired."

Whitney was about to speak again but stopped in mid-sentence when her name was called from the front of the room.

From somewhere deep within her, that voice registered a note of panic in Kelly. For an instant, she couldn't quite make out the figure standing at the door. Then, suddenly, her heart turned to stone. A cold chill swept through her body, and she shivered involuntarily.

"Oh, no!" she gasped. "It couldn't possibly be!" Kelly breathed a silent prayer. *Please Father! Oh please, don't let it be true!* But she knew before she ever uttered the words, that it was true. Vincent Rosselli had just slithered back into her life!

4

As he walked into the room, Kelly felt the color drain from her face, leaving in its wake a wave of nausea and numbness. She was finding it difficult to swallow around the knot that had formed in her throat.

It had been over a year since she had last seen Vincent, but it seemed a lifetime ago. She hadn't expected that she'd ever see him again face to face. And certainly not here—not now!

Jason's voice pierced her paralysis. "Are you okay, kid? You look like you've just seen a ghost."

Kelly thought an apparition would have been far preferable to the specter that loomed before her.

"I–um–I just don't feel very well."

On legs that swayed and shook like rubber, Kelly managed to make her way out from behind her desk and grab her coat. A cold, clammy sweat covered the back of her neck, and she prayed silently that she would be able to squeeze out the door before Vincent's attention left Whitney. She'd almost made it when she felt the iron grip on her arm.

"Well, Miss Jordan." The words were icicles piercing her heart. "Fancy meeting you here, after all this time."

She tried not to look up at him, but the hold on her arm

demanded that she recognize him. Finally, she lifted her eyes to meet the coal black ones she knew so well.

"I–I. . ." She heard herself stammering, "I thought you were in Lansing."

"And so I was." The iciness in his voice sent another shudder through her body. "Until a couple of months ago, that is. I'm working at the *Chronicle* now. I may even be their next editor. As the *Journal's* number one competitor, it looks like we may be running into each other a lot from now on."

To Kelly, the words were like a dagger. She struggled free of his grasp and, fighting desperately to regain her composure, stumbled outside to the car.

The sub-zero air helped clear her head a little, and the nausea seemed to let up by the time she got to her small apartment building. But nothing could quell the legions of thoughts, memories, and emotions ricocheting around her brain.

Her hand trembled as she turned the key in the lock. When she finally heard the click of the latch, she scrambled into the room and leaned back heavily against the door in relief.

She soaked in the familiarity of her apartment—the warm oak wood floors, the braided rugs, the over-stuffed couch and matching chair. The warm feeling of being home helped calm her down. She wrapped an ivory colored afghan around her shoulders and curled up on the blue velveteen sofa.

Kelly began to breathe more easily, and she tried to reassure herself that Vincent's appearance didn't necessarily mean anything. The terror that strangled her heart was totally unfounded, she told herself. There was no reason to fear him. Surely he wouldn't dare dredge up the whole sordid mess again.

It was all just a horrible coincidence. And despite what he said, there was no real reason for her to expect that she'd be seeing a lot of him. After all, he said he'd been here for several months already. She'd been in town herself for almost as long and hadn't run into him before.

That thought brought some comfort, but Kelly slept fitfully

that night. The periods of calm and quiet were staccatoed with bizarre dreams and haunting flashbacks all muddled together.

The cold reality of morning brought little relief. As the first rays of the sun chipped away at the icy blue-gray of the eastern sky, Kelly labored to comprehend what had happened the night before.

Relying on the structure of routine, she made her bed, showered, downed juice and coffee with an English muffin, then bundled up for work. It wasn't until she slung the camera bag over her shoulder, that she remembered her decision to visit the scene of the previous day's fire.

Grateful for something else to occupy her thoughts, she climbed in her car and headed for Seventh and Burnette.

As she turned the last corner by the abandoned railroad tracks, she saw the gutted carcass of the Freeman Factory. Yellow crime scene tape circled the rubble. A squad car and two policemen stood guard at what used to be the front entrance to the compound. Kelly parked nearby and approached them, press credentials and camera bag in hand.

Getting clearance and a warning not to enter the building, she moved toward the still-smoldering heap of metal, glass, and blackened bricks.

As she'd thought, the sight was awesome. Frozen coffins of ice encased the remains. Plumes of smoke and steam rose lazily out of the midst of muddy pools like simmering geysers waiting to erupt. Kelly shot off a roll of black and white film as she circled the building, then changed cameras for some color shots.

The sun had risen to just below the peak of the collapsed roof by this time; its shafts of cold light strained to dissipate the morning mists laying in the hollows between the hillsides. Kelly decided to back off a bit and catch a wider angle of the scene.

As she climbed a small hill about a hundred yards from the rear of the building, she was struck by the desolation before her.

The factory, distorted in the throes of death, with the mist rising out of its ashes, looked like a dying, fire-breathing dragon from some tragic Medieval folktale.

Kelly took several color shots, experimenting with different filters and exposures, looking for just the right setting, Then, suddenly, it was there. The dream shot.

The sun had edged itself into a perfect position, silhouetting the gargantuan corpse against the vapors. She fired off several shots of the spectral scene, imprinting the eerie setting in her mind as well as on film. Then, she zeroed in with her telephoto lens and kept snapping until the sun burst up over the top of the building and the magic was gone.

As she packed up her cameras, she turned to take one last look. A slight movement caught the corner of her eye.

Squinting against the full impact of the rising sun, Kelly peered intently at the shimmering heap, trying to get a fix on a dark object she was sure had been laying among the rubble just moments before, but she could see nothing more. It was getting late and Kelly glanced at her watch. Slinging her bag over her shoulder, she headed for the car.

"Where have you been!" Adam demanded gruffly, the moment she stepped through the doors. "Don't you know you have to be at the courthouse in less than an hour?

"I can't afford to have my reporters dragging in here whenever they feel like it. If you can't make it to work on time after your late night socializing, we'll have to make other arrangements around here!"

Stunned, Kelly stood in silence. For an instant she contemplated turning around and marching out the door. Then, looking around the room and seeing everyone but Jason, it suddenly dawned on her what was going on.

She turned a steady eye toward Adam's cold, steel-gray ones. "I'm sorry I was late Mr. Wentworth. But I was down taking pictures at the fire site. I assure you, my personal life has nothing to do with it. Now, if you'll excuse me, I'd like to get started on this roll of film before I have to leave."

Tossing her coat over her chair, she grabbed the canister of black and white film and headed into the darkroom. Whitney gave her a sickeningly sweet smile as she passed, gloating over the skirmish that had just occurred, but Kelly had neither the time nor the desire to respond this morning.

When she came out a short time later, leaving the proofs to dry in the darkroom, Kelly notice that Jason had arrived and was in the midst of a heated discussion with Adam in his office.

"I tried to cover for you." Whitney said in a syrupy voice. "Why, I even offered to cover the courthouse assignment for you this morning, but you know Adam, he just jumped to all kinds of conclusions." Whitney gave a short, wicked little laugh.

"Personally, I think it's just great that you and Jason hit it off so well together. I can't honestly think of any two people who deserve each other more. If you want, I can talk to Adam and straighten him out."

"I think you've done quite enough already, thank you." Kelly retorted.

She threw on her coat, picked up the camera bag and whirled around at the exact moment Vincent Rosselli walked through the door. Although taken aback, Kelly was more prepared to face him today than she had been the night before.

"So, we meet again." Vincent's narrow black eyes darted from Kelly to Whitney and back again in a conspiratorial manner.

Determined to take command of herself and the situation, Kelly fixed her eyes on Vincent, sizing him up.

At first glance he seemed to be very much as she remembered...middle-aged, medium height, a little paunchy in the stomach. But on closer examination, she could see that he had aged considerably. There were many more lines in his swarthy face. His straight black hair was thinning, and the ebony eyes she had always remembered as being sharp and cunning were now bitter and weary.

He took a puff on his cigarette, then threw it to the floor, grinding it out with the heel of his shoe. He squinted back at her through the haze of smoke.

It was obvious to Kelly that his presence there was no fluke. Whitney had probably arranged it all.

Undaunted, Kelly collected the rest of her equipment and without a word to either of them, left. But her face burned at the tittering she heard from the two of them as she walked out the door.

Kelly lingered at the courthouse longer than necessary after she wrapped up the assignment. She had used a roll of black and white film on Judge Perkins, then, remembering she still had a few shots on the color roll, decided to finish it off on the stately elm trees that stood etched in ice on the courthouse square. She hoped that if she delayed long enough both Vince and Whitney would be gone by the time she got back. Her strategy only half-succeeded. Vince was gone, but Whitney was there and just as acrimonious as ever.

Jason sat at his computer terminal, an obstinate, bull-headed expression on his face. Adam glowered in his office. The only one who had anything even resembling a smile on her face was Maggie. She was perched near the coffee maker trying to keep out of everyone's way.

Kelly grabbed her mug from the counter and poured herself a steaming cup of black coffee.

Maggie was staring at her the whole time. "Well, when are you going to fill us in?" she finally asked.

"About what?" Kelly tried to sound casual.

"For crying out loud, Kel! What is going on around here? First I hear that you and Jason are becoming a hot item…then you both show up late this morning and have this big fight with Adam…and then that Vincent What's-His-Name hangs around all morning stirring up trouble. What gives?"

31

"Nothing gives!" Kelly snapped. "A lot of people around here are making a lot of assumptions and jumping to a lot of wrong conclusions. You know, if some people would just keep their noses out of other people's business and get all the facts straight before they go around spreading rumors, there wouldn't be any problem at all!"

Kelly regretted her words the minute she said them. The hurt in Maggie's face didn't help.

"Wait, Mags. I'm sorry. I didn't mean to take my bad mood out on you."

She gave a short, weary laugh and shook her head. "You know what's really ironic? Jason isn't even a part of it. We just had burgers together last night here at the office while we discussed the arson case. That's it, pure and simple. We didn't even leave together. I have no idea where he was this morning or why he was late."

"Then why are you so uptight?"

There was a strained pause when nothing would come out of her mouth. "It's Vince."

"Vince? Whitney's friend?" Maggie gave her an astonished look. "You know him?"

"Unfortunately, I used to work for him. The man is trouble—with a capital T."

Whitney sauntered over in time to hear Kelly's last remark.

"You're a fine one to talk about trouble!" she taunted.

Trying to avoid a fight, Kelly turned and walked back to her desk. She set her coffee down, then went to collect the drying photos from the darkroom. As she switched on the red light overhead, she gave a little gasp. There, floating in a pool of foul smelling liquids, were the remains of her photos. Someone had dumped a hodgepodge of chemicals all over them, leaving little more than a melted mess behind.

best work in the bargain. Maybe we could go back down to the Freeman Factory in a day or two and reshoot."

Kelly looked up at him, surprised. It was the first time she'd seen him show any kind of concern toward any one else.

"Thanks, Jason. But that may not be necessary. It occurred to me while I was cleaning up that I still have some undeveloped color film in my camera with pictures on it from this morning. I was going to use them for my personal portfolio, but they might work for the paper."

"Oh...well...that's great. Would you like me to help you develop them?"

"I think I can handle that myself. But if you really want to do something for me, you could get me my coffee. I could use something to warm me up. I'm just freezing." Kelly shivered.

"It's probably a reaction from the shock of everything that happened," Adam soothed. "Here, take this."

He stood to remove his jacket and draped it around her shoulders, tenderly combing out a few stray locks of hair at the nape of her neck with his fingers. She shivered at his touch but hugged the heavy gray herringbone coat close, nestling in its woolen warmth. He swung a chair around and sat down next to her.

A minute later, Jason was back with the coffee. After he left, Adam turned to Kelly, taking her hands in his. They were like ice, and Adam stroked the chilled flesh, warming the slender fingers with his hands.

"Are you sure you're all right?" he asked.

His eyes fastened on hers and again she felt a tremor sweep through her, only this time, she knew, it wasn't the cold.

"I'm positive. Really." She pulled her hands away from his. Cradling the hot cup of coffee, she sipped slowly from it, half hiding behind the mug.

"I fired Whitney." Adam spoke without emotion.

Kelly looked up in surprise. "Oh, Adam, do you really think that was best? I mean, we have no proof that she was the one who actually destroyed my photos."

"It's like I said before, it really doesn't matter if I have proof of that or not. Her attitude the last couple of months has been detrimental to the whole staff and that, alone, is enough to justify my actions."

"I'm afraid firing Whitney is only going to make matters worse," Kelly said. "What if she tries to take legal action? She *is* a competent journalist. And she *has* managed to do all the work she's been assigned...."

"Why are you defending her?" Adam asked, irritation apparent in his voice. "If you're going to defend anyone, I'd think you'd want to defend yourself.

"I don't know what went on between you and Rosselli, and you don't have to explain if you don't want to, but Whitney threw some pretty nasty accusations against you. I think I know you well enough to believe you wouldn't deliberately hurt anyone, but those kinds of charges could start people talking."

"I'm not defending her," Kelly insisted. "And I didn't defend myself because there wasn't any reason to...."

Kelly saw the confusion in Adam's face and hesitated, but his kind eyes gave her the courage to continue.

"You see," Kelly explained, "shortly after I received Christ as my Savior, my dad said something to me that changed my whole attitude toward dealing with difficult people and difficult situations. He told me that a Christian never, ever has to defend himself because if he's done something wrong, no defense is possible—and if he hasn't done anything wrong, no defense is necessary.

"All that's required of us is the truth. And the truth is...I *did* file harassment charges against Vince Rosselli. But I never asked for a promotion or any special favors from him nor did I threaten him in any way. And, frankly, I'd just as soon drop the whole subject.

"Vince has chosen to tell Whitney a different version of what really happened and she's chosen to believe him. Nothing I say is going to make a difference."

Kelly could see the skepticism in Adam's face. "I know you think I should have said something...should have denied her accusations. But what would that accomplish?

"She wasn't going to believe me. I wasn't going to change her mind. And like you said before, those people who know me, know that I would never make such charges without a good reason.

"If I'd gotten angry and gone on the attack, it would only have convinced Whitney that I'm guilty of Vince's accusations.

"I believe the Bible has a better answer." She turned to Proverbs 25:15 and read, "'By forbearance a ruler may be persuaded, and a soft tongue breaks the bone.'

"Being defensive never makes things easier—even when it's obvious you're being treated unjustly. The best thing you can do is turn it over to the Lord. God will settle our accounts if we trust Him to. He's proved it to me before. I expect He will in this situation, too."

Adam sat silently listening to her words. "For your sake, I hope you're right, because when Whitney gets mad, she's like a fighting bull. Her pride's been wounded now. She'll be looking to get even with you. She'll go charging off after you, and she won't care who she hurts in the process. My own instincts say to take action now, before she has a chance to do too much damage. She's vindictive."

Kelly smiled. "I know a lot of people scoff at the idea of waiting patiently on the Lord and not returning evil for evil. But, I think if you give God a chance to work things out, you'll eventually see that He knows what He's doing. That's what I'm counting on."

"Is that what you meant about 'persuading the ruler with forbearance'?" Adam grinned, his silver eyes twinkling. "I suppose that's what you've been using on me."

Kelly could feel the color rising in her cheeks. Fortunately, a mild commotion in the next room bailed her out of having to reply. She could tell from the laughter that Kevin and Maggie were back from lunch.

"Guess I better get back to work." She gave a weak smile. "Looks like the crew's back. I'm sure they're gong to have a field day when they find out what happened while they were gone."

Kelly pushed her chair away from the table and handed Adam's coat back to him, but as she rose to her feet, her head began to spin crazily and she grabbed for the edge of the table to steady herself. Adam was instantly at her side.

"I must have gotten up too quickly." Kelly shook her head. She attempted to take a step, but the dizziness increased and she sat back down in the chair with a thud.

"You're not going anywhere but home, young lady," Adam ordered. "I'll see to it personally if I have to. You wait right here, and I'll get Jason to cover for me."

He returned in a minute with her coat and purse. "Everything's set." He helped her on with her things. "Kevin's going to do layout, and I called in a part-timer to fill in for Whitney. Just take it easy and lean on me while I take you out to my car. I don't think you're in any shape to drive home."

Kelly tried to protest, but she was grateful for Adam's strong arm around her. She swayed and would have fallen without it. The control and power in his every movement had a calming effect on her.

Kelly's head was still swimming as Adam settled her into the rich brown leather seat of his cream-colored Cougar.

On the ride home, she tried to reassure him, and maybe herself as well, that it was just the pressures of the past few hours and her lack of sleep, coupled with little or no food that was making her so lightheaded. But as she talked, she realized a deep drowsiness was settling into her very bones. As they drove along, her talk became more of a babble, then faded off altogether. By the time they got to the apartment complex, each movement was a struggle for Kelly.

She stumbled up the first few steps, but finally, Adam swept her up into his arms and carried her the rest of the way up the short flight of stairs to her second floor apartment. As he gently set her down, she leaned back against the wall. She was aware that he had asked her something, but she couldn't concentrate any longer and just shook her head numbly.

"Kelly...Kelly, look at me." Adam cupped his hand under her chin and brought her face up to meet his anxious eyes. "I think you'd better see a doctor. Maybe I should take you to the hospital."

"No. No. Please, I'll be all right, I just need to lie down for a while," Kelly murmured. "Here. Let me get inside and rest." She struggled to find the keys in her shoulder bag, but it seemed to weigh a ton and as she fumbled with the clasp, she spilled the contents all over the floor.

Supporting Kelly with one hand, Adam fished the keys out from among the pile of makeup, film canisters, and the remaining paraphernalia with the other. After unlocking the door he helped her settle on the couch.

"Now, Kelly, listen to me. I think I should call a doctor. Where's your phone? Kelly...did you hear me? Do you have a doctor here in town?"

"What..." Kelly fought to understand what Adam was saying. "No. No, don't call anyone, I'll get Dr. Manning." She tried to rise but Adam laid a hand on her shoulder.

"Just stay put, I'll phone him."

"You don't have to do that..."

"It's all right. I don't mind."

"No...you don't understand." It was getting harder and harder for Kelly to focus. "He's right across the hall. Apartment 208."

"Okay. Okay. I'll go get him. Just don't try to get up, all right?" He waited until she nodded her assurance.

It seemed only a moment before the bespectacled gray-haired doctor stood beside her. Adam quickly explained as much as he knew about Kelly's sudden illness, then stepped back to let Dr. Manning examine her.

After the initial vital signs had been taken, Dr. Manning turned to Adam with a puzzled look. "Mr....um...Wentworth, was it?" Adam nodded. "Would you happen to know if Kelly took any medication today?"

"No—I don't think so. Why?"

"Well, her pupils are constricted and from everything else you've mentioned, it sounds like she could have taken some kind of sedative...Valium perhaps or more probably a barbiturate of some sort." He turned back to Kelly.

"Miss Jordan..." From somewhere deep inside a growing fog, Kelly felt him pat her gently on the cheek. "Kelly..." She groaned in response. "Kelly, try to listen. It's very important. Do you remember taking any pills today? Maybe you thought you were taking aspirin or a pain reliever and took something else by mistake."

"No. No pills." She groaned.

"Are you absolutely positive? Anything at all that might have looked or tasted strange?"

Kelly struggled to remember what she had consumed since she had gotten up that morning.

"Just coffee," she whispered, "that tasted bitter."

Dr. Manning turned to Adam. Kelly heard genuine alarm in the doctor's voice as he asked, "Do you think someone could have slipped her something in her coffee?"

"I don't know, but I'll find out. I'll call the office immediately and have Maggie send Kelly's coffee mug to the crime lab."

"Kelly? I think you should come to the hospital overnight so we can keep an eye on you."

"No. Please, Doc. I just want to go to sleep right here. I want to stay home." Kelly fought back the waves of unconsciousness and forced herself to semi-alertness. "Okay? Please?"

The doctor turned to Adam with an exasperated sigh. "She sure is stubborn....What's the matter?"

Adam set the phone back down on the counter, a frown on his face. "Any other day I'd have to ask our receptionist a dozen times to pick up empty coffee cups and pop bottles around the office. But today—the only day I would have appreciated a little forgetfulness—she's already straightened everything up. The coffee's gone, the mug washed, the evidence—destroyed." Adam let out a low sigh, then added, "I guess my talk about cleaning house worked a little too well.

"So," he turned back to the doctor, "what do we do now?"

"Well, there really isn't much we *can* do. I could take her to the hospital, but she's already fighting that idea." As if to confirm that statement, Kelly started to protest.

"I can't really make her go. All her vital signs are in good shape, but I won't leave her here alone. Can you stay with her? If not, I'll have to call for an ambulance. I've got another patient waiting for me right now, otherwise I'd stay with her myself."

"No, Doc, don't worry about that. I'll stay with her if you think she'll be all right."

"It doesn't look like she could have taken very much of whatever it was. She should just sleep it off in a couple of hours or so.

"I'll look in on her again when I get back. If she seems to have any trouble at all breathing or with nausea or any other kind of pain, call the hospital immediately and ask for me. Other than that, I'd say, just let her sleep."

He wrote the hospital number down and left it next to the phone on the kitchen counter. Adam thanked him and walked him to the door.

After Dr. Manning left, Adam removed his jacket and tie, then sat down opposite Kelly in an old wooden rocking chair.

"Looks like you've really done it this time, girl," he said softly.

Kelly was still aware enough to respond with a weak, "What?"

"Gone and made a couple of dangerous enemies, that's what. Sometimes I think you deliberately expose yourself to situations where you know you're going to get hurt. It's as if you purposefully lay open your heart, knowing full well someone is going to rip it to shreds."

"And that concerns you?" Kelly managed a smile.

"It concerns me a great deal," he scolded her and then, just as the overwhelming urge to sleep claimed her, Kelly thought she heard him add, "Perhaps more than it should."

6

Kelly moaned and turned toward Adam, trying to snuggle closer to the throw pillow she clutched in her arms. Adam rose and quickly searched the tiny apartment.

He found a pillow and an afghan in her bedroom. Gently, he lifted her head and nudged the pillow beneath the crown of cinnamon curls.

He tucked the afghan around her, and as he arranged the creamy folds of hand-knit cloth about her, soft petal-like fingers curled around his own.

The sensation caused him to freeze for an instant, his gaze transfixed on the slender fingers now securely entwined about his hand.

He swayed slightly, indecision flecking his eyes.

Then, seating himself on the edge of the sofa, Kelly's hand still clinging to his, he brushed back a feathery wisp of hair from her brow, tracing the arch with his thumb.

She turned her head toward him slightly, revealing the pronounced lines and deep hollow of her elegant neck. He watched, mesmerized, as the blood pulsed rhythmically through the carotid artery, now lying exposed at the juncture of her jaw line and throat.

Conflict revealed itself in every muscle of his body, every action he took. He made a move to stand but then relaxed by Kelly's side. His grip on her hand tightened.

Silently, he stroked his fingers through the loose curls. Then, ever so gently, he slipped his hand beneath her neck and pulled her close.

He held her for what seemed like an eternity, his heart throbbing heavily. He wrapped his arms more tightly around her, rocking her gently. Kelly curled closer to him. He brushed her hair lightly with his lips, then as if suddenly awakening from a dream, released her.

He stood, muttering to himself, "Wrong! Wrong! Wrong! I'm not falling in love with this girl! I can't be. She's one of my employees. Now stop it!"

Clearly shaken, Adam paced the floor, running his hand again and again through his thick hair.

Determination replaced the look of confusion on his face. "I simply won't allow it," he mumbled to himself.

Adam rested his hands on the sill of the living room picture window. The sun was slowly setting behind the early winter landscape, casting long gray shadows across the lawn.

"Maybe I shouldn't even be here," he argued with himself. "Maybe I should just call Maggie and have her come stay with Kelly." He rubbed the back of his neck as he turned his gray eyes toward the now quiet form on the couch.

He stood there staring at her for the longest time, lost in thought, remembering the day she had moved in.

She'd been a wreck, dressed in blue jeans and sweatshirt, cobwebs in her curls and dust smudges on her forehead where she had brushed back the hair from her caramel-colored eyes. She had been so serious and pragmatic about directing the whole moving operation that day; Adam had told her that his Marine Corps Drill Sergeant hadn't been as rough on them as she was.

That comment had sent Kevin into a hysterical rendition of

a wind-up wooden soldier frantically following orders and tripping over himself, all at the same time.

At first Kelly had pursed her lips and pouted, "I'm not that bad!" But the more she protested, the harder Kevin laughed until he finally got her to crack a smile and let a series of suppressed giggles spill out. At the same time, she was ordering Kevin to stop laughing at her which only made him salute, say, 'Yes, sir!' and hoot all the louder.

Finally, she had picked up a sofa cushion and flung it at him. It missed him easily by three feet, but it hit Adam squarely between the eyes. Kelly had turned a fascinating shade of crimson, and Adam milked her embarrassment for all he could.

Then, he had surprised himself by grabbing the cushion and hurling it back at her. It had been a trigger. All three of them had collapsed into reckless abandon with pillows and cushions flying from one end of the apartment to the other. It took them almost as long to clean the place up after their pillow fight as it had to move Kelly in the first place.

He finally moved and resumed his seat in the rocker opposite her. For several minutes all he could hear was the quiet creaking of the chair and the tick-tock of the kitchen clock.

The harsh jangle of the telephone brought him out of his deep introspection. Kelly never stirred as Adam talked with Jason, calling to check on a few items for the *Journal*.

When Adam finally finished the call, he noticed that the sun had set and the apartment was in near darkness. He snapped on an overhead light in the kitchen and began searching for something to eat.

After finding an apple and a couple of slices of cheese, Adam made his way back to the living room where he promptly tripped over Kelly's shoes. Switching on a lamp beside the chair, he picked them up along with her coat and shoulder bag, remembering just then, that half of its contents were still scattered in front of her door.

He quickly retrieved the littering of film canisters, tissues,

47

and other odds and ends, then took everything to the bedroom and laid them on the large brass bed which took up the majority of floor space in the connecting room. It was draped neatly with an ivory and mauve colored bedspread matching the afghan he had used for Kelly.

The room itself wasn't very large, but there was a good-sized alcove next to the bathroom that had been used in the past as a dressing room. Kelly had fixed it up as sort of a mini-studio.

Framed samples of Kelly's work were everywhere and on a small desk along one wall of the alcove lay the artist's portfolio Kelly had mentioned earlier.

Adam hesitated, then moved over to the desk. He unwound the drawstring on the catch. Carefully he removed the leather case from its heavy bindings and unsnapped the clasp. Pushing aside a few papers on the desk, he cleared an area and set the album down.

Seating himself on the cushioned secretary's chair, he arranged the portfolio in front of him and switched on the gooseneck lamp standing at the corner of the desk. A moment of indecision made him pause and he almost put the book back. Then, he placed his hand back on the bindings. Adam pulled the album closer to him, then drew a quick breath as he flipped open the cover.

The heaviness of drugged sleep clung to Kelly's eyes as she fought to wake up. She tried to lift her head, but the fog billowed around her. Mentally shaking off the sleep, she raised herself to a half-sitting position. Still dazed, it took all of her concentration to focus on where she was and what had happened to her.

Comforted by the realization that she was safe in her own apartment, she tried to piece together the events of the day. The first thing that came to her was a haunting picture of Vince and Whitney.

At first she couldn't remember why that distressed her, but then Whitney's words came echoing back. She recalled that

Jason and Adam had also witnessed the scene, and there was some recollection of Adam helping her into his car, but her memories became distorted and fragmented after that. Had Dr. Manning come?. . .Had he mentioned something about pills?. . .She couldn't quite remember.

Kelly slowly swung her legs out from under the afghan and settled on the edge of the couch. With great effort, she wobbled to her feet, gripping the back of a chair for support. Her head spun wildly for a few seconds, but quickly cleared, giving her the courage to take a few hesitant steps. She glanced at the kitchen clock: 6:00.

Focusing with all her might, Kelly strained to recall what had happened after Adam brought her to the apartment. Gradually, bits and pieces began falling into place.

Dr. Manning had definitely been there. He had seemed to think she had been drugged. The idea seemed preposterous at first, but what other explanation could there be?

Distinct impressions of Adam's presence flowed into Kelly's memory. Had he held her? Or had she dreamt that part? She couldn't be sure.

Through the lifting mists of her mind, she heard a rustling from the bedroom and noticed that a light was on. Someone had stayed with her. Kelly breathed a prayer of relief and thanks.

She called out softly, but there was no response, so she moved across the living room, through the bedroom to the arch of the alcove. The sight she saw there made her heart stop. Adam was sitting at her desk intently poring over her personal portfolio. A knot of dread tightened in her stomach. She hadn't shown those pictures to anyone since. . .since Vincent.

There, before Adam, in a kaleidoscope of color, lay a whole world of iridescent images. Hot air balloons, fields of spring flowers, and colorful carousel horses danced off the pages.

There was a tiny tyke, his face lit with laughter, carrying a squirming, oversized puppy in his arms.

Another shot, taken in the midst of a swirl of yellow butterflies, caught scores of them in mid-flight. The sun gave them an ethereal appearance as the light shone through their translucent wings.

On the last page of the section, a portrait of a circus clown showed his arms cradling a young girl with braces on her legs. Happy-faced in a big, orange smile, the clown's greasepaint could not cover the tracks of a single human tear that traveled down his bright white cheek. Printed below the portrait was:

"Permit the children to come to Me; do not hinder them; for the kingdom of God belongs to such as these. Truly I say to you, Whoever does not receive the kingdom of God like a child shall not enter it at all" (Mark 10:14-15).

On the next page, a black and white photo captured a lonely willow at the edge of a still pond, weeping in the morning mists.

There was a photo of a storm over the Badlands and a fairy tale scene shot from below the arch of a countryside bridge with sunbeams breaking through the shimmering leaves of young aspen trees.

A myriad of panoramas followed: desolate deserts, cactus flowers in full bloom, rolling meadows laced with yards of daffodils and dewy baby's breath.

Kelly watched Adam leaf through the pages once, twice, the expression on his face growing more intense with each perusal. And time and time again, he came back to that picture of the little girl and the clown and the caption that lay beneath it. Sorrow etched his face. Then, suddenly it went stone cold. After that, he just sat staring blankly out into nothing.

Kelly couldn't keep Vincent's words about those very pictures from sweeping through her brain. Amateurish, he had called them. Stupid and silly.

"They're absolutely worthless," he had told her. "No one wants to see this kind of fluff anymore! People want realism. History in the making. Not this juvenile human interest garbage!" His words still stung—even in memory.

She had tried not to give Vincent's opinions too much

credence after everything that happened, but at the time, it was hard not to be hurt by his criticism. After all, he had been a savvy and sophisticated journalist in his day, and he couldn't have become an editor without some knowledge of public opinion. As much as she would have liked to dismiss his disparaging remarks, they still burned in her heart. From that moment on, Kelly had been too afraid to show them to anyone else.

If she had been devastated at Rosselli's condemnation, the thought of being judged by someone with the credentials and professional standards of Adam Wentworth terrified her. And the look on Adam's face didn't help matters.

His features had taken on a gray, melancholy cast—a hardness, maybe disillusionment. Had he been so disenchanted with her work, Kelly wondered, that now he regretted hiring her?

Kelly's mind was racing. Her first impulse was to leave. But as she turned to go, she heard him move. He had gotten up from the desk and wandered over to the far side of the studio.

His attention had been caught by a large photograph Kelly had hanging on the wall directly opposite the desk. It was a self-portrait.

In the picture, Kelly was posed against a burgundy backdrop and was dressed in a deep burgundy wraparound dress with rose petal sleeves. The only lighting was a candle she held in her hand. Adam drew closer to it.

"Fascinating!" The word whispered from his lips.

"What is?" she asked.

Startled, Adam swung around. "Kelly! I didn't know you were up yet."

"Obviously. Now what's so fascinating?"

Looking chagrined, Adam turned back to the portrait. "The eyes," he said simply.

"What about them?" Kelly studied the picture, trying to see it from Adam's perspective. All she saw was their reflection of the flickering candlelight.

Adam seemed hypnotized by them. "They seem to mirror an

inner glow, a fire of their own. They're warm and inviting, yet seem so wise and caring."

Tearing himself away from the photo, he focused his attention back on her real-life eyes.

"They remind me of someone else, too."

"Who?"

At first it looked as if Adam wasn't going to answer. But then, taking his wallet, he took a picture from it and handed it to Kelly.

"My wife. . .I mean, my late wife, Helen."

The photo was of a golden-haired woman. Kelly studied it for a moment.

It was the strangest thing, she thought, the two pairs of eyes were entirely different. Helen's were cobalt blue. . .Kelly's honey brown. Helen's had turned up slightly at the corners and been framed by wispy blonde lashes. Kelly's were deep set and accentuated by sharply arched brows that seemed to put a question at the end of each glance. Yet, there was a fire burning within them; the openness, the honesty were exactly the same.

Kelly took a step toward him to hand back the photo. As she did so, she swayed slightly, then steadied herself against the desk.

Adam was immediately by her side.

"You shouldn't have tried to get up so soon," he scolded as he led her back to the living room.

"Afraid I'd catch you poking around my pictures?" she teased.

"Maybe. You know, you really surprised me with those photos. Your work at the paper is entirely different from what you've expressed in your personal portfolio. It's a side of you I've never seen before. Your work at the *Journal* is so crisp and clear cut and these—they're so. . .so. . . ."

"Soft and superficial?" Kelly finished, her lower lip quivering in anticipation of the criticism she was sure to follow.

"I was going to say dynamic—energetic—even. . .impassioned. In fact, I was going to ask you why you're working at a little local daily like the *Journal* when you could be doing very nicely on your own, working anywhere in the country."

Kelly looked up wistfully at him through her long dark lashes. "If you're saying that just to be kind, you really don't need to bother. I'm not going to faint on you again, so you don't have to worry about hurting my feelings." She looked away, tears welling in her eyes.

With a free hand, Adam caught her chin between his thumb and forefinger and turned her face to meet his gaze. Looking directly into her brown eyes, he seemed to see the mounds of misgivings there.

"Kelly," he said softly, "when I hired you, I knew that you were very talented and highly professional. But it wasn't until I saw your portfolio just now that I realized what an extraordinary gift you possess." He drew closer to her.

"You see things as few people see them. And more important, you have the capacity to make others see them, too." His voice took on a huskiness. "I don't know why you'd be afraid for me to see them."

Kelly swallowed hard. "I'm afraid because...because those pictures are a part of me...and because I care what you think of me. If you don't think very highly of them, then I know you can't think very highly of me. And I–I just don't think I could stand it if that was the case."

It was out. Kelly's heart rose to stick in her throat. A teardrop slipped silently down her cheek, and Adam brushed it away with his thumb.

Until that moment, Kelly hadn't realized just how close she was to him. Her pulse rate jumped at his touch.

Adam drew a long breath and held it, then reached out and pulled her close. His eyes were full of longing and desire, but, they were also filled with fear.

Suddenly, his hand pressed in at the small of her back and the other cradled the nape of her neck, drawing her face up to meet

53

his lips. He brushed her mouth lightly at first, almost tentative in his approach. Then with profound tenderness, he found her lips again.

There was a hunger in the kiss—a keenness to it—that made her stop breathing for an instant. It sparked an electrical charge that triggered every ion in her body.

Then, without warning, Adam pulled roughly away.

His hands still gripped her upper arms but the movement snapped her back to reality and she also stiffened.

His head was bowed so that she could not see his face as he grappled for control. His breathing was labored and his voice shook.

"I'm sorry," he whispered. "I shouldn't have done that." His hands, still tightly gripping her arms, trembled ever so slightly.

"As an employee of the *Journal*, you are my responsibility. I didn't mean to take advantage of the situation like that." His voice was hoarse and strained. "I hope you can forgive me."

Kelly forced her emotions back down inside her heart. In her head, she knew that he was right to back away and knew that she should, too, but in her heart, she fought against his words.

"Don't worry about it," she faltered. "I shouldn't have gotten so emotional over a few pictures like that. I'm the one who should apologize."

When he finally looked up at her, Kelly knew that an invisible curtain had fallen between them. A cavern of silence spread between them and in the middle quavered a repelling force that drove them apart.

Adam straightened, then released her. Kelly responded in kind and for a long awkward moment, they stood mute, trying to reason out what had just occurred. When the doorbell rang, both were visibly relieved for the interruption.

7

It was Dr. Manning. He gave Kelly a quick once-over and seemed pleased with the results. His only prescription was to feed her, put her to bed, and call if she needed anything.

Adam insisted on fixing her supper and Kelly, too tired to argue, acquiesced. He scrambled up some eggs and toasted a couple of English muffins. They ate in silence for several seconds, then Adam broke the stillness.

"We need to talk about what happened today."

"What do you mean?" Kelly cocked an anxious eyebrow.

"The drugs, of course," Adam answered.

"Oh, that." Relief filled Kelly's voice. "I don't know what to say. I suppose someone could have slipped me something. But that seems a bit dramatic, don't you think?"

"Do you have a better explanation?"

"No. But it's hard to believe anyone would hate me enough to drug me. Besides, if someone really wanted to hurt me, he could have given me a much stronger dosage."

"True enough. He could have killed you," Adam replied.

"Well, now, that's a cheerful thought," Kelly said sarcastically.

"Sorry, I'm just trying to figure out why this happened.

Whoever did it had to have a reason. Maybe it was revenge. Or perhaps you were getting in someone's way. If we can figure out why you were drugged, maybe we can figure out who did it."

"I don't know. You'd think if someone wanted me out of the way, he—or she—would have used something besides a tranquilizer. All that did was put me out of commission for a while."

"So you don't think it was Whitney or Vince?"

"I don't see what they had to gain."

"Unless they wanted to scare you," Adam suggested.

"Well, they certainly did that," Kelly agreed.

"What if it *was* Vince or Whitney?"

"I don't know. I wasn't really hurt. And Whitney's no longer around." Kelly shrugged. "Without any proof, I guess I'd try to forget the whole thing."

"Just forgive and forget, huh?"

"Sure. I suppose. I mean, there really isn't much else I could do."

"Most people I know can't forgive that easily."

"It's only difficult to forgive if you make it difficult, Adam. The Bible *commands* us to forgive each other just as God forgives us."

There was a momentary pause and Kelly wondered if she'd said too much. But exploring the expression on Adam's face, she saw a glimmer in the gray eyes that registered interest, maybe even a challenge.

"You mean to tell me you can forgive someone—anyone— just like that?"

"You mean, could I forgive *Whitney* that quickly?"

"Maybe."

"Listen, I'm not saying I *feel* forgiving all the time, or that it's easy. Our human nature—a sinful nature—doesn't want to let go of those feelings. But, when you stop to think about it, forgiving isn't an emotion. It's an action. An action the Lord requires of us if we're to receive His full blessings. If you ask

God to help you forgive someone, He will, and then the feelings will follow."

Adam mulled that over a few seconds, but a look of uncertainty clouded his face.

"Some people don't deserve to be forgiven." It was a statement, not a question, and Kelly knew instinctively they were no longer talking about Whitney Hewitt.

"You're absolutely right, Adam. Some people don't deserve forgiveness."

Adam looked up, surprise obvious in his face.

"I didn't deserve God's forgiveness when I came to Him. But He gave it to me anyway. Because He loves me. There wasn't anything I could have done to earn that forgiveness, but God had already sent His Son to die in my place to pay for all the sins I committed. Now, the least I can do for Him is to forgive others the same way He forgave me...even when they don't deserve it."

Adam contemplated her words. "You mean a person should forgive others even if he's been deliberately hurt and the guilty party makes no attempt to rectify the situation?"

"I believe it's best to forgive even if the offending party doesn't ask for or want your forgiveness. Not only for what it does for the other person, but for what it can do for you.

"Forgiving is a freeing experience. When you can't forgive, you build up bitterness and resentment. The word resentment comes from the French word that means 'to feel again'. If you can't forgive, you can't let go of the past. Then you relive past hurts over and over again. In effect you keep alive all the pain and anguish and sorrow."

"But what if a person has done something so terrible you can't forgive him?" Adam said. "What if he's done something that's destroyed another person's life? How is it possible to forgive someone like that?"

"It's a matter of perspective, I guess. From God's point of view, not even the worst of us is beyond His forgiveness.

Christ's sacrifice on the cross covers all sin if we ask.

"It also helps to remember that there isn't a single person on earth who was born looking to have people hate him. Each one of us was born with a desire to be loved—a God-shaped vacuum in our hearts that only His love can fill.

"Some might try to deny it, but it's there nonetheless. The thing is, in their search for love, some people get all twisted up in their thinking and in their emotions so that they can't tell the difference between attention and real love. So they end up doing anything just to get people to notice them.

"Or else they'll try to convince themselves that they can substitute other things for it, like money or power or revenge. The trouble is—the emptiness is still there. Only the Lord Jesus Christ can make a person feel complete."

There was silence again.

Finally, Kelly said, "If you're interested, why don't you come to our Bible study tomorrow night? We're studying forgiveness."

"I don't know. . . .It's been such a long time. . . .I'll think about it." Adam pushed himself away from the table. He glanced at the clock. "I didn't realize it was so late. Guess I better get going. Pick you up tomorrow morning at 8:00 if you want."

"Please, don't bother. I can hitch a ride with Maggie. She just lives a block or two over."

"You sure you're going to be okay tonight? I hate leaving you alone like this."

"You worry too much, Adam." Kelly grinned.

Adam's face grew somber. "I don't think I am in this case. Someone deliberately drugged you. We don't know who or why, and they're still out there. This time, it turned out all right, but promise me that you'll be very careful the next few days. Maybe you should have Maggie stay with you."

"I hardly think that's necessary. This is a pretty safe neighborhood and besides, Dr. Manning is right across the hall."

Adam seemed to be reassured by that and left. Kelly called out a quick "thank you" as he walked down the steps, then turned around to the silence and loneliness of her apartment. Her mind teemed with a multitude of questions, concerns, and emotions.

There were so many unknowns darting around in her head: Who had drugged her that morning and why? How was Whitney going to react to her dismissal? But through all the questions, one memory occupied her mind—Adam holding her, kissing her.

Why had he taken her in his arms? And why had he released her so suddenly? More importantly, why did it matter so much?

Memories of another time and place crept into her mind and a warning registered. She felt a prickling at the back of her neck that told her she had come dangerously close to making a big mistake. Experience told her the best thing for everyone was to make sure her relationship with Adam remained on a purely professional level.

Adam evidently felt the same way. He had made it abundantly clear that all he felt for her was a responsibility to protect her. She was his employee and nothing more. Still, the memory of his embrace sped through all the warning lights.

"Stop it!" she screamed at herself. "What happened tonight must never—ever—happen again!" But, even as she said the words, she was hoping that it would.

8

It took Kelly a long time to fall asleep, but when she did, she slept heavily.

In the morning, she woke groggy and confused, almost convinced she'd dreamed the whole thing. She found it difficult to get up out of bed and snuggled deeper under the covers when the alarm went off. Dressing was a chore and, on several occasions, she found herself staring absentmindedly out the window instead of preparing for the day ahead.

The winter sky hung heavy with the threat of snow and Kelly's mood matched the gray clouds. She didn't feel much like talking and was grateful that Maggie kept up a steady one-sided conversation during their drive to the office. Apparently everyone had heard that she may have been drugged, and Maggie was full of the latest developments concerning the previous day's events.

Kelly glanced around the newsroom as she entered, fearing yesterday's episode would place her in an uncomfortable limelight. She was relieved to find, instead, everyone hard at work, and no one paid any great deal of attention to her except to ask how she was feeling.

In fact, the sameness of the office setting seemed almost eerie as Maggie and Kelly took their respective places. After everything that had happened, Kelly half-expected the offices to be in shambles. But the only thing out of place was Whitney's empty chair, and Kelly's reluctance to look into the Managing Editor's glass-enclosed office.

Kelly tried to remain calm when he came out to talk to the staff. Forcing the memory of his embrace from her thoughts didn't seem to do much to quiet her hammering heart.

If Adam sensed anything, however, it didn't register in his face. His tone of voice was a bit more crisp than usual, but Kelly couldn't be sure it had anything to do with her. It could be that he was just anxious to reassign Whitney's duties to the rest of the staff.

Most of the details assigned to Kelly were rather routine. Jason would handle the extra feature assignments, Kevin would get a shot at doing some hard news reporting, and Maggie got the task of clearing out Whitney's desk.

"Just send the box with her things to her apartment," Adam directed. "Use one of the couriers."

"You know, she was here last night," Maggie said, "with that Vince guy. She said she wanted to clean out her desk right then, but Jason caught the two of them snooping around and kicked them out."

Anger flashed across Adam's face. "I don't want her coming in here for any reason. Get her things out of here as soon as you can. And if she asks, tell her she'll get her last paycheck by mail."

It didn't take long for the entire staff to settle in to their new responsibilities. With the holiday advertising rush under way, no one could afford the luxury of taking extra time getting acquainted with a new routine.

Kelly had just finished arranging her schedule for the day and had walked over to the front desk to consult with Maggie on her lunch plans when the front doors exploded inward.

The blast shot Maggie about a foot in the air as she whirled

61

around to meet a red-faced, boiling mad George McClanahan.

He fumed past the two of them, a morning issue of the *Journal* clenched in his white-knuckled fist. He stormed directly over to Jason, cracked the paper across his desk and lit into him with the fury of a two-ton tornado.

"I thought you understood the meaning of 'off the record'!" he bellowed. "I told you this was confidential!" He pounded the paper with a pudgy finger.

"From now on, you want any information—any information at all—you speak to Vince Rosselli over at the *Chronicle*—'cause he's the only one I'm talking to!"

He stepped back, still puffing with anger. "Where's Wentworth?" he demanded.

Without waiting for an answer, he marched over to Adam's office and slammed open the door. Adam had risen when he heard the angry voices. Now he pulled McClanahan into his office, shutting the door behind him.

Every eye in the outer room was riveted on the two angry men. The thick glass of Adam's office muffled their conversation, but no one had to hear the exact words to know what the two were saying.

Kelly had moved back to her desk, but couldn't keep her eyes off Adam's face. At first, only indignation and resentment registered there. Suddenly, his expression turned to disbelief—then shock.

She saw him form the words, "You're crazy," then, slowly, he turned toward the large glass window. His gaze swept the room until they stopped on Kelly. George McClanahan had also shifted his attention to her.

Kelly stood transfixed. Adam's hand went down to the phone on his desk. He picked it up and punched a button, his crystal clear, gray eyes never leaving her. The buzzer on her phone went off. She picked up the receiver as if it were a rattlesnake.

"Kelly, I need to see you in my office—now." Adam's deep voice clipped off the words.

Kelly was aware that her fellow employees were watching her, and curiously, she felt as if she were doing the same thing. She felt her body responding to Adam's instructions, but somehow her mind had detached itself from the physical reality. If she hadn't been so conscious of everyone's eyes, she might have believed she was sleepwalking.

She walked into Adam's office and quietly closed the door. Adam pulled out a chair for her and motioned for her to sit. She did so, but it was as if her body was responding on its own volition and through no will of her own.

"McClanahan has some questions he wants to ask you, Kelly." Adam was saying. "I want you to know right now, though, that you don't have to answer anything if you don't want to. And, if you do choose to talk to him, we can wait until I can arrange to have a lawyer present."

"A lawyer!" Kelly gasped. "What do you think I've done that I would need a lawyer?"

"Tampering with criminal evidence, for starters," George McClanahan interjected.

"I didn't tamper with anything," Kelly replied. "I don't know what you're talking about."

Adam sat on the edge of his desk. "Apparently, some evidence uncovered by the state crime lab from Tuesday's fire is missing. It was located the other night behind the building. When they came to pick it up the next morning, it was gone. The police assigned to the factory reported seeing you at the site yesterday morning. The investigating team wants to know if you saw anything while you were down there."

"No. Not that I can think of. I mean, I don't think so. All I saw was a pile of burnt bricks."

"You sure of that, Miss Jordan?" McClanahan turned an accusing eye towards her. "You didn't, by any chance, happen to come across something you felt could get you a scoop for your paper and just decided to keep it to yourself until you could break the big story?"

"I most certainly did not!" Kelly sputtered. "Besides, how would I know what was incriminating evidence from among that pile of debris? It seems to me, the only one who would know is whoever started the fire!"

She stopped, realization striking home.

"My point exactly," the state fire investigator said flatly. "So, just where were you Tuesday afternoon?"

"That's enough, McClanahan!" Adam broke in. "I'm not going to have you badgering my reporters like this."

"It's all right, Adam. Really." Kelly spoke up. "I received the news of the fire at the same time everyone else did, between 4:00 and 4:30. And I was right here when we got word."

"But the fire had been burning for quite some time before it was discovered. Were you in the office all afternoon?"

"Well, of course not. I was out on assignment part of the time. But half the population of Bingham wouldn't be able to account for their whereabouts at that time either."

McClanahan changed the direction of his attack. "You're rather new to the area, aren't you, Miss Jordan? Been here a couple of months now, haven't you?"

Kelly nodded.

"About the same time these fires have been occurring, I would say." His voice dripped with allegations.

"All right! That's it!" Adam clenched his jaw, the corded muscles in his neck tightening. "I've had enough of your insinuations. If you want to talk about coincidences, perhaps we should talk about your own circumstances. Seems to me we didn't have any trouble the nine months you were out of town retraining for this new position. Then, three months ago, you come back to Bingham and, bam, more arson fires. Care to explain that?"

"I've got no motive," McClanahan snapped.

"And Kelly does?"

"It's not the first time Miss Jordan's name has been connected with a suspicious incident. I just got some very interesting reports from Detroit."

Kelly turned white, but held her ground. "Then you also know the police investigating the accident cleared my name."

Adam looked up in surprise, but asked no questions.

"Maybe so," McClanahan said, "but that doesn't necessarily clear you in this incident. Seems to me, being the new kid on the block, you could get yourself a lot of publicity for coverage of a string of arson fires. Especially if you know when and where to go looking for them."

"And it seems to me the city council didn't feel Bingham needed a fire investigator until this arsonist started up again." Adam's eyes burned with accusations.

McClanahan's red face puffed up once more as he turned on Adam. "You want motives? Then let's take a look at yours, Wentworth. Ever since your wife died, you've done everything in your power to ruin me. What better way to get rid of me once and for all, than to make it look like I can't solve these arson fires? Well, I've got news for you! I *am* going to find this arsonist! No matter who it turns out to be!" His gaze zeroed in on Kelly, then he turned and stomped out the door, slamming it behind him.

Kelly was in a daze. "He can't possibly believe that either of us is involved in this! Adam, what is going on here?"

"I don't know, Kelly. I really don't know. I guess he's frustrated, and he's taking it out on the *Journal* because Jason got him to admit he hasn't got a clue who the arsonist is. I'm only sorry he chose to drag you into the middle of this."

Concern crept into his face. "You sure you didn't see anything suspicious yesterday down at the factory?"

"Honest, Adam. I can't think of a thing. . .except. . ."

"Except what?" Adam's silver eyes fastened on her.

"Well, just as I was leaving yesterday's shoot, I thought I saw something move down at the bottom of the hill. But I didn't have time to check it out." Kelly shook her head. "It was probably just my imagination. Besides, it's too late to do anything about it now."

"Maybe not," Adam remarked. "Didn't you say you had some other photos of the factory?"

Kelly's eyes lit up. "Yes, the color ones."

"Well, maybe you managed to capture something with your telephoto lens you didn't notice with your own eyes. I think I'd like to take a look at that film if possible."

"You bet! I'll develop it right away!"

Kelly went back to her desk and checked the spot where she usually kept her camera bag. It wasn't there. Then, remembering she'd left it behind when she'd gotten sick, she turned to Maggie, who was busy cleaning out Whitney's desk.

"Mags? Have you seen my camera bag?"

"I think the guys stuck it in the darkroom," Maggie directed.

Kelly found it under the cabinet and made a quick search for the film. She came up with several canisters, but none of them contained the type of film she'd used for the factory fire.

"Now don't panic," she told herself. After all, her camera bag was only one of several places she kept film. She checked her desk next.

She was about to give up when it finally came to her. Her purse! Whenever she ran out of room in the camera bag, she tended to shove extra canisters in her shoulder bag. She dumped out the contents of her purse and sifted through the odds and ends. Again, she came up empty-handed.

"You didn't leave it in your camera, did you?" Adam called to her as he made a general inspection of the inner offices. "I thought that's what you said yesterday when you first mentioned you'd taken them."

"I don't normally leave a spent roll in the camera." She called back. "I like to put a fresh roll in right away so I'm ready in case of an emergency. But it's worth a try."

She took out both cameras and double-checked them. One contained a fresh roll of black and white film. The other, to her surprise, was empty.

"That's odd," she commented. "I haven't forgotten to reload a camera in ages."

She quickly put in a fresh roll, then thumped down in her chair, baffled and discouraged. Irritation twisted her mouth.

"I can't for the life of me figure out where it could be!"

Just then, Maggie called from Whitney's desk. "Take a look at this!"

"Mags!" Kelly jumped to her feet. "Did you find the film?"

"No. Something even more interesting!" She fished around the bottom drawer for a few seconds, then pulled out a little orange and brown container.

Adam moved over to inspect her discovery. He pulled off the white cap and spilled out a half dozen of the tiny yellow pills into his hand, then turned the bottle to get a better look at the label. "Valium," he said. A hush fell over the room.

For a long time, no one spoke. There really wasn't anything to say. Adam seemed hypnotized by the bottle he held in his hand. Kelly stood with her mouth open, unable to form any words.

"I was hoping I was wrong about Whitney," Adam finally managed to say. "I really didn't want to believe she was capable of this."

Jason let out a low whistle, stunned, as were the rest of the group, by the discovery. "You gonna prosecute, Kelly?"

His words brought her back to her senses.

"Prosecute her. . .for what?" she stammered. "For having a bottle of Valium in her desk? I hardly think that's a punishable crime."

"Good grief, Kelly! It's obvious what this means. Whitney must have been the one who slipped you the pills."

"There's no solid proof of that, Jason. You're a reporter. You know this is purely circumstantial evidence. Other people had access to her desk and to the pills."

"But no one else could have known they were there...or would want to hurt you," Jason insisted.

"Really?" Kelly questioned. "I can think of at least one other person that fits that bill."

"Vincent Rosselli," Adam murmured.

"We may never know the truth," Kelly added. "Anyway, it's over and done with. Whitney's gone and I doubt Vince will be a problem as long as she's not around. Perhaps the best thing for all of us is to put the incident behind us and get on with the work at hand."

She turned around sharply, deliberately letting everyone know that as far as she was concerned, the conversation was over. "I'll have to look for the film later. I've got a meeting to cover in half an hour."

Kelly straightened up her desk and gathered her photo equipment together. The thought of the missing film nagged at the back of her mind, but she had more pressing items on her agenda at the moment.

She was in and out of the office the rest of the day. It had started to snow, the first heavy snow of the season, and she was called out on a couple of minor auto accidents on top of her regular duties. When she got back to the office late that afternoon, Maggie and Kevin were getting ready to leave.

"We still on for tonight?" Kevin asked.

"Oh, right! The Bible study. I'm glad you mentioned it. I almost forgot."

"You better not," Maggie grinned. "You promised to buy dinner. Remember?"

"Yes, I remember. How about if I pick up a pizza, and you can meet me at my place about 6:30. That'll give me a chance to wrap things up here and get my clothes changed. Kevin, you come too, okay?"

"Sounds good to me." Kevin rubbed his hands in anticipation. They left and Kelly returned to her desk.

Jason had also gone for the day. Adam was still in his office. Kelly noticed he had the bottle of Valium sitting on his desk. She finished her work quickly, then hesitantly rapped on

Adam's door as she put on her coat.

At his invitation, she opened the door and stuck her head inside. "I–I just wanted to let you know I was leaving now. Is there anything else that needs to be done?"

He shook his head. She turned to leave but stopped. "Kevin and Maggie are coming over for pizza tonight, then we're all going to the Bible study. . . .If you'd like to come for dinner, you're more than welcome."

He looked up at her, his gray eyes reflecting the white fluorescent lighting. They seemed to brighten for an instant, but the glow quickly faded. He glanced back down at some papers on his desk, pretending to be involved with them.

"I don't think that would be very wise," he said softly. "An employer really shouldn't be socializing with his employees."

Kelly felt as if the wind had been knocked out of her. *There's no doubt about it now,* she thought. *Adam really doesn't feel anything for me but responsibility.* Her heart sank at the realization.

Kelly could have kicked herself for hoping, if even for an instant, that Adam felt more. He had made it clear that he would not get involved with one of his employees. And, of course, he was right. If anyone knew how dangerous mixing business and personal lives could be, it was she.

"Well, the Bible study starts at 8:00 if you want to come on your own," Kelly offered. "I really think you'd find it very interesting."

There was no response.

You idiot! she yelled at herself as she turned to leave. *Why are you pushing him so hard? Every time you say something stupid like that, he clams up. Why can't you just leave well enough alone?*

She walked out the front door into the snowy night, her head pounding with recriminations.

9

Kelly heard Kevin enter the foyer downstairs as she popped the pizza in the oven to warm it up.

"I'm up here!" she called out to him. "Be careful not to trip up the steps. Another bulb burned out in the stairwell, and it's pretty dark in here."

"No problem! We'll just call the Super!" Kevin laughed at his inside joke.

When Kelly first moved into the apartment, she had discovered a number of items in disrepair. When she approached building maintenance, she was informed that they couldn't do anything without "approval from the Superintendent." That included anything from furnace repair to watering the potted plants that decorated each floor's landing. After making dozens of phone calls and being given the royal runaround, she discovered the official superintendent listed on her lease lived somewhere in the Bahamas.

With his usual chivalry, Kevin had tackled a number of the minor projects, for which Kelly had bestowed upon him the title of "Superintendent In Absentia." Ever since then, he often ribbed her about expecting a condo in the Caribbean as payment for his services.

"The Super will have to fix it some other time," Kelly laughed, "because if he doesn't get up here right now, he'll miss out on his part of the pizza."

"Oh no, he won't!" Kevin bounded up the steps.

Maggie arrived a few seconds later.

"Man, there must be 4 or 5 inches of snow out there already!" she declared as she shook off her snow-covered coat and wiped the melted flakes from her glasses. "Even for the Upper Peninsula this is early for blizzard conditions. Weather reports say we might get snowed in."

As the pizza was being passed around and the pop was flowing, Kelly realized how truly grateful she was for these two new friends, especially after the last couple of days. Their light-hearted banter lifted her heaviness and that was something she definitely needed. It didn't even bother her when they needled her about her recent encounters with Adam and Jason.

"So, how did things go here yesterday. . .all alone with the boss?" Kevin teased. "You really think you can handle both Jason and Adam?"

"Very funny," she retorted, then gave a crooked smile. "If you really want the truth, I don't think I'll have to handle either one of them. They're both too involved with their work to be interested in me."

"I don't know about Adam," Maggie spoke up, "but I don't think that's true of Jason. I think he really likes you, Kel. He's been awfully interested in you lately. He keeps asking me all sorts of questions."

"Oh really?" Kelly raised an eyebrow. "Like what?"

"Oh, you know. Where you like to go. . .what you like to do . . .if you're *involved* with anyone. . . " she said with emphasis. "I think he's kind of jealous of all the attention you pay Adam. He told me today he was going to see if he could get Adam to team you two up together on the arson case. He said it was because he admired your work, but I think he just wants to spend more time with you."

71

"You do, do you?" Kelly blushed. "Tell me, Mags, how is it you seem to now so much about what Jason thinks? He sure is cool to everyone else. How come he confides in you so much?"

"Oh, I thought you knew!" Maggie answered matter-of-factly. "Jason and I lived with the same foster family for a while. Neither one of us liked it there very much so we just naturally turned toward each other for company.

"Jason's about as close as I've ever come to having a real brother. I know he's kind of hard to get to know, but he's had a tough life. Deep down, though, he's really a nice guy. He's the one that got me my job at the *Journal*."

Kelly was taken aback. She wanted to know more, but didn't want to push for details. And a quick glance at the clock showed it was time to go.

They all decided to pile into Kevin's car. Kelly enjoyed riding in his semi-restored '57 Chevy. It was Kevin's pride and joy. He'd been working on it for several years, putting every spare dime and minute into its restoration. He'd painted it fire engine red and dubbed it The Cherry Bomb. It had become quite a conversation piece around town.

Now, as they drove through the dark streets, Kelly imagined herself back in the late fifties when this car symbolized the age of the carefree teen. She could just see herself pulling up to a drive-in, ordering burgers and fries.

She smiled at the images the car conjured up. Maybe she could do a photo lay-out on The Cherry Bomb come summer. They'd all get a kick out of that. She was plotting out the project in her head when the car skidded.

Kevin had the Chevy under control instantly, but the movement jolted Kelly upright and her heart flip-flopped. That distinct sensation of being out of control triggered the sounds of squealing tires, breaking glass, and a hideous thump in her mind. Kelly literally shook her head to dispel the images. . .then forced herself back to reality.

Every muscle in her body had automatically tensed, and she

had to will herself to breathe again. She shivered as she stared out into the blackness. It was snowing heavily and she studied the flakes carefully, intentionally focusing on them to the exclusion of all else.

"We probably won't have very many at the Bible study tonight," Kevin observed.

Including Adam, Kelly added to herself, her thoughts turning back to the sad, haunting eyes of the Managing Editor as she'd left him at the office. She saw again the loneliness in his face ...heard the coldness in his voice at her invitation. Once again she felt the sting of Adam's reference to proper employer/employee relationships.

Why did that bother her so much? she wondered. After all, Adam *was* her employer and she agreed with him in principle about keeping the two separated. She had, in fact, used almost the same words herself not too long ago. But why did that seem so different? Was it because the words had been directed at Vince Rosselli at the time?

Kelly felt a creepy-crawly uneasiness wiggle down the back of her neck. From outer appearances, the two situations didn't look all that different—a boss and employee becoming entangled in a relationship.

But it was *different!* Kelly argued with herself. Vincent wasn't a Christian. She hadn't wanted to get involved with him. Secondly, he'd abused his authority and taken advantage of her compassion. Kelly had only wanted to be Adam's friend...but that was before last night.

Now, she'd begun to question her own motives and intentions. In all honesty, she knew she'd felt a deep attraction for Adam right from the start.

Had she really wanted a relationship with him all along? Had she unconsciously manipulated circumstances to make that happen? Was she really any different from Vincent? Had she been guilty of deceiving herself and others in order to get what she wanted?

73

Suddenly, a disturbing thought shot through Kelly's mind. Did Adam see her as she saw Vince? Was that why he had become so cold after their kiss last night? If that was the case, then there was a good chance Adam would be suspicious of anything she had to say. How she wished now that she hadn't pushed him so hard about coming to the Bible study.

I'm sorry, Lord, she apologized silently. *I want your will, but I was trying to insist on mine. Help me. Keep my emotions from getting in your way.*

When they arrived at the church, there were only two other cars in the parking lot. As they walked into the fellowship hall, they realized that only four others plus the study leader, Pastor Conrad, had braved the bad weather.

Their Bible study that night centered on the parable of the indebted servant from the 18th chapter of Matthew. They had just begun reading when they heard a noise at the back of the room. Kelly looked up quickly to see Adam come in. Their eyes met and Kelly's heart stopped for a second, terrified that he might turn around and leave. But just then, the instructor called out to him and invited him to join the group.

"Nice to see you again, Adam," Pastor Conrad greeted him.

Adam nodded hello, then chose a chair several seats away from Kelly and settled rather uncomfortably into it. Someone handed him a Bible and for the next 45 minutes he sat listening, never saying a word.

As their discussion on forgiveness progressed, Adam seemed to be absorbing it all with deep interest.

Maybe this is just what he needs, Kelly decided. *It would be normal for him to feel a lot of bitterness over the dreadful fire that killed his wife. And if there is someone Adam needs to forgive, maybe he can do it now and put an end to this whole tragic episode.*

Adam seemed engrossed in the discussion, but during a lull in the conversation, he suddenly spoke, and Kelly's heart sank.

"All this talk of forgiveness and compassion is one thing," he began. "But tell me, what good does it really do to be a Christian? My wife was a Christian. She loved the Lord with all her heart and what did that get her? Dead. That's what it got her. And me? I lost the woman I loved and felt sure God had led me to marry. Now why would God allow that to happen to her?"

His comment struck the group like a thunderbolt. Words, responses, emotions...all seemed to hang in mid-air. There was silence for a moment. Then Pastor Conrad answered Adam's question with one of his own. "Why do you want to know, Adam?"

It was Adam's turn to be speechless. His eyes narrowed as he stared at the pastor.

"I only ask," the study leader said in a kind voice, "because most people who ask God why He does or doesn't do something aren't really interested in knowing why, they only want to argue with Him. They want God to change His mind about a certain event."

Kelly could see Adam's face tightening. What would happen if Adam got mad and walked out? She struggled to say something, to soften the words that were being spoken, and yet, something inside her held her still.

"I just don't think it's fair, that's all," Adam was saying. "I mean, if being a Christian doesn't protect you from something awful happening to you, then what good is it?"

"Are you saying that Christians should never have problems?" the pastor asked. "If that was the case, then we would all worship God out of fear or for some favor we thought He would do for us. . .not out of real love. Not even the Apostle Paul was free from pain or suffering."

"I see your point." Adam's face relaxed. "But I still don't understand why my wife had to die. Couldn't God have prevented it?"

"Sure. If it would have been a part of His overall plan, He could have changed the situation. God has the power to do anything. But I think you're missing an important truth here.

"Your wife was a member of this congregation for a long, long time. I knew her well. As a Christian, she knew that her soul would never die, and she would go to live with the Lord when her time here on earth was ended. Your wife is with God right now. And I have a hunch that, given a choice, she'd rather be there with Him, than here with us.

"I know that doesn't make the pain any less for you, but you will see her again someday, if you were sincere when you received Jesus Christ as your Lord and Savior.

"You made that choice several years ago, Adam. You said then, that you wanted to let the Lord take over your life. I think you meant it, but I wonder if you ever followed through on that commitment. It isn't enough just to *say* 'I believe.' You have to *act* on your commitment. God expects our obedience, worship, trust. The Bible says that faith without works is dead."

"What kind of 'works' are you talking about?" Adam probed. "I give to charity. . .obey the law. . . .Is that what you mean?"

"That—and more. . .like forgiving others when they hurt you. . .like our Bible study was talking about tonight. But that's only the beginning.

"Once you've taken care of the past, you need to surrender every part of your present and your future to the Lord. You can't expect God to straighten things out in your life if you don't give Him control of it. And only you and God know if you've done that.

"I'd like to talk to you about it some more when we both have a little more time," he finished. "Right now, I think we better dismiss the Bible study before we all get snowed in." He left it at that, inviting Adam to come to church on Sunday.

Kelly couldn't read Adam's face in response to the pastor's words, but she prayed that the Holy Spirit would work in his heart. After the group broke up, Kelly didn't know if she should approach Adam or not. Adam solved the problem by waiting for her just outside the door.

"Kelly, could I talk with you for a minute?"

Kelly hesitated. "I came in Kevin's car. I'll see if they can wait a few minutes for me."

"That's okay," Adam said, "I can give you a ride home."

Kelly nodded and tried to act casual about the invitation, but she didn't like the way her heart was tripping over itself at his suggestion.

She reminded herself of the promise she'd just made to God about keeping her emotions under control, but she couldn't help feeling excited at the prospect of helping Adam find the peace he so obviously needed.

She called over to Kevin and told him about the arrangements. Kevin gave her a knowing smile, nodded, and left with Maggie.

The parking lot cleared in a few minutes leaving Kelly and Adam alone together. They waded through the accumulating snow to his car and settled into the luxurious seats. He started the engine to warm the heater, then sat in silence for a moment or two.

Finally, Adam said, "I've always liked Pastor Conrad. He's honest. Direct. I like that in a person. If he would have given me some kind of soft-sell routine tonight, I don't think I would have believed him."

Kelly nodded in agreement.

"But, I'm still really mixed up about the forgiveness part," he continued. "I've been doing a lot of thinking about what you said last night. You're probably right. I probably have been living too much in the past. I know I've allowed the fire that killed my wife to dominate my life. But, I can't seem to forget what happened. It was such a terrible thing—sometimes I think it was too terrible for anyone to forgive."

"But you can *learn* to forgive," Kelly interjected. "What's done, is done. You can't change what happened by being angry. For your own sanity, Adam, you must find some way to forgive the person responsible for starting that fire!"

Adam turned to her. "Oh, no! You've got it all wrong! It's me

77

I'm talking about. I don't think that God could ever forgive *me*!"

Kelly was stunned. "I don't understand."

"I just feel. . .responsible, that's all. Don't you see, Kelly? Helen was always a better Christian than I was. She's the one who always went to church while I worked overtime at the office. She's the one who committed her life to witnessing to others while I worked on building my career. Why, she was even the one who introduced me to Christ and what did I do? Nothing. Absolutely nothing. Helen didn't deserve to die, Kelly. I'm the guilty one. I couldn't even pray for her while she lay dying. I never learned how."

Suddenly Kelly did understand. Apparently, Adam saw Helen's death as a punishment for *his* sins. In that instant, Kelly knew the only one Adam really needed to forgive was himself.

"God's forgiveness doesn't depend on how good you are or how religious you act," she said, struggling to find the right words. "It only depends on Christ. All that really matters is your relationship with Him. If you believe in Him, then whatever it is you think you've done to deserve God's wrath has already been taken care of. God took all His anger at us out on His Son at Calvary. Because Christ took the punishment for our sins, God forgives us and welcomes us into His family. That's the whole point of Jesus' death and resurrection."

"I understand that, Kelly. But that was before I accepted Christ's blood as the covering for my sins. But what about now? I mean, what about after a person becomes a Christian, and knows right from wrong? What if he commits a terrible sin after he's received Christ as his Savior?

"Let's say he does something out of pain or selfishness that hurts another person and there's no way to fix it? How can God forgive that?" There was a quiet desperation in Adam's voice.

Kelly stared at him in astonishment. His question sounded more like a confession, and Kelly had to wonder what this unforgivable sin was that Adam had convinced himself he'd committed. She stopped herself from asking him, though, knowing he needed assurance now more than anything else.

"You're assuming that God can't separate the person from the act. He may disapprove of what we've done, but He won't hate the person. He brings the sin we've committed to our attention. And usually we have to pay the consequences of our wrong actions. But that doesn't mean God won't forgive that person. First John 1:9 says, 'If we confess our sins, He is faithful and righteous to forgive us our sins.' "

Adam's face grew pensive.

"God's forgiveness is already available for all sinners," Kelly continued, "including the Christian who strays from God's will. All you have to do is confess the sin, turn from it— change your actions or thoughts—and the Holy Spirit will help you do that.

"Of course, if there is something you can do to make the situation right, then by all means do it. But if it's impossible to make restitution, then you have to let go of the guilt. . . .Satan ties us up in guilt feelings." Kelly had to pause, to keep her voice from trembling. "If we let guilt destroy us—or anger or bitterness or any sin—then our service for God is nullified or weakened. You must simply trust that God loves you enough to offer His forgiveness to you with no strings attached."

Adam's countenance fell. "But what if I've pushed Him too far? What if He's stopped loving me?"

"Oh, Adam." Kelly's heart went out to him. "That can't happen. We have to believe His promise to always love us no matter what—and to always forgive us when we ask Him to."

A look of utter desolation swept Adam's face. "I don't think I have that kind of faith, Kelly. In fact, I don't know that I have any faith at all. And if I don't have that faith, then maybe I'm not a Christian after all."

The words were spoken with an emptiness that tore at Kelly's soul. Her heart sank to the pit of her stomach.

"Paul told Timothy, in his second letter, that even when we

are too weak to have any faith left, God still keeps His promises. And in the eighth chapter of Romans, God promises that nothing can separate us from His love.

"Listen to me, Adam. God loved you so much, He was willing to sacrifice His only Son. If He was willing to go that far for you, do you really think He would abandon you now? Or that He isn't in control of everything?"

Kelly's challenge was met with silence.

"I can't make you believe in God's promises, but whether you believe it or not, God *does* love you and *will* forgive you. Take a chance, Adam. Just ask Him. What have you got to lose?"

Kelly searched Adam's face, but all she saw was doubt. He didn't say anything for a long time. Finally, he mumbled something about getting her home before the roads got any worse.

He put the car in drive and turned toward Kelly's section of town. Like a heavy cloak, despair slipped around her shoulders. The night closed in around them, and the only sound was the steady, muffled. . .slap, slap. . .slap, slap. . .of the windshield wipers.

10

There was another fire early the next morning. A minor one in an abandoned and condemned apartment complex located in the seedier part of the city. Jason called Kelly at her home and told her to meet him at the fire site. By the time she arrived, the action was pretty much over but Jason was, as usual, right on top of things.

He instructed Kelly to take several shots of the lower level where most of the damage had occurred, then sent her winding up an old fire escape on the backside of the dilapidated building where he was sure he'd seen George McClanahan disappear a few minutes before.

"I think he's hot on the trail of something important," Jason insisted. "I've got to know what it is. I can't get within 50 feet of him without him bolting, so I'm depending on you to find out what he's up to."

Kelly was only too happy to tail the petulant Fire Investigator. His recent accusations had created a new resolve within her to find the person responsible for the fires.

Cautiously, Kelly started up the rickety, wrought iron stairway, her boots tapping out step after step as she climbed to the second story. The fire had not reached this portion of the tumbled-down tenement, but the age of the fire escape combined with the icy conditions made her climb a precarious one.

"That's it," Jason encouraged her. "You're doing just fine. It's the next window up. I'm sure I saw him enter there."

She was only four steps from the designated window when she heard Adam's booming baritone from below.

"Just what in the world do you two think you're doing? Kelly! Get down here, right now!"

Kelly whirled around at the sound, then grabbed for the railing as she lost her balance for a second. Adam's face went white, and he made a dash for the steps, but Kelly called out to him that she was okay.

She looked back at the window she had been about to enter, then down at her boss. It didn't take her long to decide that if she wanted to keep her job, she'd better do as Adam ordered.

Slowly she descended the steps and within two minutes she was safe on the ground.

"I've come to expect such foolish behavior from Kelly," Adam was yelling at Jason, "but I thought you had more sense than to pull a stunt like this."

"It wasn't a stunt!" Jason railed back. "We were doing our jobs! Getting your story for you!"

"No story is worth the lives of my reporters."

"Is that what you're really worried about?" Jason accused, "or is it that you just don't want us digging too deep—finding out too much. Maybe you're just jealous that we've been able to uncover more about these fires than you have. Or maybe you're just mad because I'm getting all the attention and glory for my arson series."

"That's enough!" Adam shouted. "I'm not going to dignify your idiotic accusations with an answer. I'm still in charge here and if you want to continue working for this paper you'll keep those kinds of remarks to yourself. Now get back to the office and turn in your story—or you might find yourself asking Vince Rosselli for a job."

Jason stomped away in disgust.

Kelly was appalled at Jason's accusations. Yes, he was angry—and with some reason. He'd been working night and day on this case with few results. Adam's interference was the last straw for him. But Jason's frustration didn't justify the kind of verbal attack she'd just witnessed. She was about to apologize for Jason's behavior, but Adam didn't give her a chance.

"As for you, young lady..." Adam turned on her. "You nearly gave me a heart attack, crawling around on that brittle old building like that. Just what did you think you were trying to prove?"

"That I'm capable of doing my job." Kelly's brown eyes snapped. Her cheeks grew hot with indignation as she felt her resolve to remain calm melt away. She was about to add more when she got her first good look at his face.

Adam looked shockingly worn and haggard. He ran his fingers through unkempt hair, then rubbed both hands across his unshaven face. It was obvious he hadn't gotten any sleep. Kelly felt a twinge of empathy for him and softened her tone.

"I'm sorry I lost my temper, Adam, but I'm not used to getting yelled at for doing what I get paid to do."

"You get paid to take pictures, not risks," he snapped, then paused as if ashamed of how harshly the words had come out. He bowed his head a second to regroup, then looked up.

"Listen, Kelly, I'm sorry I yelled at you, but good grief, girl, you just about scared me to death. I just can't understand why you find it necessary to dig so deeply into this arson investigation. You're not responsible for solving this case. McClanahan is. Let *him* take the risks."

"But maybe I *am* responsible," Kelly responded. "If I hadn't lost that film from the Freeman Factory fire, we might have solved this case days ago.

"Ever since I lost that film, Jason and I have been trying to come up with something...anything...that would give us a clue to the identity of the arsonist. This time, we had a good solid lead and before we could check it out, you stopped us."

"What lead?" Adam demanded.

"Jason saw McClanahan go in there." Kelly pointed to the third story window. "We were sure he was up to something."

"Well then, let the police handle it. And from now on, you're to keep me informed on everything concerning this case. Do you understand?"

"Yes, sir," Kelly replied.

"And you're not to place yourself in any more of these dangerous circumstances. Is that clear?"

"Perfectly," she answered, with a touch of sarcasm.

"Good. Then I'll see you back at the office in 15 minutes."

Kelly watched him leave, puzzling over his reaction. It wasn't like him to blow up like this about work. She could understand Adam's concern over the safety of his people, but there had been much more emotion in his voice than simple fear or worry. No, his volatile response indicated something much deeper. Kelly couldn't quite put her finger on it, but she had a feeling it had to do with what had happened after the Bible study.

Could Adam be struggling with what she'd said to him? Was he trying, in his own way, to straighten out his relationship with the Lord?

Kelly recalled the look on his face as they'd driven home last night. His reaction had frightened her. She had seen in his eyes the despondency, the dejection, the despair of someone without hope, and she didn't know how to counteract that.

Back at the office, Kelly questioned him about it.

His voice was flat and even when he told her he didn't care to discuss it, but his eyes reflected turmoil in his heart.

Those eyes only convinced Kelly that his reaction earlier had been due, in large part, to their discussion about forgiveness.

She tried to talk with him about it a couple of times during the next few days, but he always changed the subject. At one point, he even told her flatly that it was none of her business. Kelly still cringed from how much that had hurt.

After that, Adam immersed himself in his work, concentrating his full attention on the arson investigation. Very often, she'd arrive at work to find him hunched over a stack of papers in his office and realize he'd been there all night.

During the day it seemed as if he never had more than a minute to talk with her about anything, including business. It became painfully evident that Adam was doing his best to put some distance between them.

Still, there were moments when Kelly noticed a wavering in his voice when he was close to her. And, on a couple of occasions, when she had been deeply absorbed in a particular project, she'd looked up to find him studying her...his jaws clenched. . .those cool gray eyes filled with an unfathomable expression.

Although she couldn't read the look, it gave Kelly the distinct impression that Adam's recent display of formality was nothing more than a paper-thin facade covering a storm of emotion.

The storm erupted the day of the Tri-County News Award Nominations.

Kelly and Jason had been assigned to cover the press conference being held at the *Chronicle*, and Kelly was not looking forward to it, mainly because Vincent Rosselli would inevitably be there.

He had been making quite a name for himself around Bingham. George McClanahan had made good his threat to give exclusive rights concerning the arson case to Rosselli and in doing so, he had plunged Vincent into the limelight.

"Vince will be insufferable if he receives a nomination," Kelly remarked to Maggie as she gathered her equipment together. But, then she quickly apologized for the critical remarks.

If she was to get through the briefing, she'd have to keep a lid on her feelings toward Vince. She decided the best thing was to go do her job as quickly and as inconspicuously as possible, avoiding trouble at all cost. That plan might have worked, too, if Jason hadn't called in sick at the last minute and forced Adam to accompany Kelly to the conference.

"Of all times for Jason to get sick!" Kelly complained.

"Yeah," Kevin chimed in. "How come Jason always manages to worm his way out of these things?"

Maggie glared at him, the color rushing to her cheeks. "What do you know about it?" she snapped at Kevin. "If he says he isn't feeling well, then he isn't feeling well."

Kelly had never seen Maggie so worked up over a simple comment. "He was only teasing, Maggie." She tried to smooth things over.

"Yeah, you don't have to take my head off," Kevin added.

Maggie backed off. "I'm sorry," she said. "But Jason really hasn't been feeling well lately, and I'm worried about him."

"I really *am* sorry," Kevin said contritely. "Is it something serious?"

"No. No, it's just something that crops up every once in a while. That's why he's missed so much work lately. I'm sure he'll be able to get it under control, though."

"You know, we could pray for him," Kelly suggested.

Maggie shook her head vehemently. "No. Don't do that. He would be angry with me if he knew I'd said this much. Just forget it." She turned back to her work, obviously determined to change the subject. Kelly was running late, so she dropped it as she left with Adam.

Vince was laying in wait for Adam and Kelly at the press conference, Whitney draped on his arm.

"Mr. Wentworth," Rosselli said in feigned formality. Adam turned to avoid the pair, but Vincent headed him off.

"I'd like you to meet the newest member of our news team." Vince flashed a sardonic smile. "I know you two already know each other, but aren't you going to welcome Whitney to the staff?"

Adam turned a steady eye toward him. "I'm sure Whitney

will fit in perfectly with the caliber of reporters the *Chronicle* hires," he said evenly.

Whitney was not amused. Her jade eyes flashed, and she would have responded to his comment, but the announcements began. Adam and Kelly made their escape to the other side of the room.

John Edwards, publisher of *The Tri-County Chronicle* and the host for this afternoon's press conference, took his place at the podium.

"Ladies and gentlemen of the press," he began, "I want to welcome you to the 16th Annual Tri-County News Award Nominations. I know you're all anxious to find out whose names will appear on the ballots this year, and we'll get to that in just a moment. But first, I'd like to take this opportunity to make a special announcement of my own.

"As most of you know, I've been running the *Chronicle* for over 25 years and my wife has finally said 'Enough!' She says she's tired of me tearing off in the middle of the night, driving through blizzards and tornadoes just to get an exclusive.

"Now, we all know that's an exaggeration. . ."

Polite laughter rippled through the room.

"Nevertheless, she *is* my wife and in deference to her wishes, I hereby announce my intention to retire at the end of this year.

"My successor hasn't been chosen yet, but we have a couple of very good candidates, and we plan on making that announcement in a few weeks at the Awards Presentation. So, to all you hopefuls out there, watch your step, and may the best one win. Now, on with the program."

"Did you know about this?" Kelly questioned Adam as she snapped a few pictures of Mr. Edwards.

"No. But it doesn't surprise me. John's been announcing his impending retirement for years now. He hasn't carried through on it, though, because he said he could never find anyone qualified to take his place. I wonder who he has in mind. . . ."

Adam glanced uneasily at Vince Rosselli. "I only hope he

has sense enough to get someone with a little integrity and not just someone with editorial experience or he'll run this rag right into the ground."

The nominations went about as Kelly had expected and, after taking a dozen or so pictures, she walked to the back of the room, bored and restless, to stand by Adam, waiting impatiently to get out of the crowd.

That's probably why she didn't realize at first that it was her name being spoken from the podium. When it finally dawned on her, she jerked up, then blushed as she realized the committee had placed her name in nomination for a photography award.

At the announcement, a wide grin broke across Adam's face. She looked at him in disbelief, then was rocked with a wave of humility and excitement as she realized that Adam must have submitted some of her fire photos on her behalf.

The gray eyes crinkled up in appreciation and delight and, in an uncharacteristic display of exuberance, Adam wrapped an arm around her and gave her a quick hug. His action surprised Kelly since his attitude the past few days had been anything but warm and friendly.

Ironically, this display of affection was not lost on Vince and Whitney. The two sidled over to Adam and Kelly as the last of the nominations were being read off.

Kelly was trying to coax Adam into letting her take a second look at the burned out apartment complex—something Adam was more than a little reluctant to let her do.

"Oh, Adam, please? The police have secured the building by now and I promise to be extra careful." She was pleading.

"If the police didn't find anything, what makes you think you can?" Adam countered.

"I don't know. I–I just feel like I need to do something to make up for losing that roll of film from the Freeman Factory fire. There has to be some clue, some little bit of information, that will help us discover who the arsonist is.

"I know you're not very pleased with Jason's attitude, but you have to admit he's a good reporter. And if his latest hunch is correct, that piece of evidence could be laying somewhere in that old tenement building right now."

"What's the matter, honey?" It was Vincent. "Doesn't your boss have any confidence in you? Maybe he just feels threatened. Doesn't want to let a woman show him up. Is that it, Wentworth?"

Kelly tried to ignore him. That wasn't so easy for Adam.

"Stay out of this, Rosselli. It's none of your business."

Rosselli laughed derisively. Adam turned back to Kelly.

"I'll make a deal with you. If you can get the police to okay it—which I doubt they will—you can go, but only if someone goes with you, okay?"

Kelly nodded her agreement.

They tried to leave then, but Vince and Whitney seemed intent on keeping them there.

Aided by the logistics of the small room and the large crowd, Whitney wedged her way in between the couple until she had Kelly positioned out of earshot of the men.

"Tell me again how I was wrong about your using Adam to get what you want," she hissed.

"I don't have to tell you anything," declared Kelly. "And it wouldn't matter anyway, would it? You're going to believe what you want to believe no matter what I say."

"That's right, because your actions speak louder than your preaching, sister." Whitney shifted her position and her tactics.

"Tell me—what did you have to do to get Adam to recommend you for an award nomination? Or did you blackmail him the same way you blackmailed Vince?"

Kelly glared up at her with hot, brown eyes. She tried to push her way past her dark-haired antagonist, but Whitney blocked her path.

"Know what I think? I think I had you pegged pretty good. Funny, though, I never thought Adam would be so meek and mousy as to succumb to your manipulations. At least Vince had the backbone to stand up to you."

"What you think is not important," Kelly countered. "The truth will be revealed in the end. When that happens, you'll finally realize what kind of man Vincent Rosselli really is."

"And just what kind of man is that?"

Kelly jumped at the sound of Vincent's voice.

"Lying. Deceitful," she spat back.

"Is that any way to talk about the next publisher of the *Chronicle*?" A diabolical gleam crept into Rosselli's eyes. She hated that…had always hated that look. He always seemed to be laughing at her, mocking her. It made her want to reach up and smack the smile right off his face.

Suddenly she wanted to hurt him. Make him pay for all the pain and humiliation he had put her through. In fact, it scared her to think just how badly she wanted to hurt him. She couldn't stop her words.

"Don't be so smug, Rosselli. You're not publisher yet. And you won't be, either, if I have anything to say about it."

"Don't threaten me," he returned, his words like daggers of ice. "You never were a match for me. Face it, Kelly. You haven't got the stomach for a good fight. You're just too nice."

Adam stepped between the two of them just then and in a commanding tone, directed Kelly to pack up her equipment. But as she reached for the camera bag, Vince grabbed hold of her wrist.

"I'm warning you, Jordan," he muttered, "keep your mouth shut."

"And I'm warning you!" Adam caught Vince's arm in a vise-like grip making him release Kelly instantly. "You touch her one more time and the fight won't be with her. It will be with me!"

Adam didn't give Vince a chance to respond. He grabbed Kelly's bag and ushered her out the door.

When they got in the car, he turned to her and took both of her hands in his. She was shaking but he didn't know it was more from her anger than from fear. Adam drew her close, holding her until he could feel her pulse rate drop.

"Kelly? You okay, now?" He brushed a stray lock away from her forehead. The concern in his voice made her heart melt, and when she looked up into his gray eyes, she was smitten with a tender aching that touched and tightened every muscle in her body.

When she assured him that she was fine, he backed away a bit, an air of gravity enveloping him.

"Has he ever threatened you like that before?" he asked.

She shook her head.

"I want you to promise me you'll tell me immediately if Rosselli ever does anything like this again. I want to know if he even phones you," he insisted. "If anything should happen to you. . ." he began, "I–I just don't know what I would do. I care . . .about you. . . ." Realizing what he said, he caught himself. "I mean, I–I feel responsible for your welfare."

At Adam's admission, Kelly's affection for him swelled, but with those final words, something inside her went flat.

"Well, you're not!" she answered in hurt and anger. "You're not responsible for me or my welfare."

She wasn't sure why she was suddenly so mad at him. Every time she seemed to be on the verge of breaking through one of his barriers, he threw up a new one.

"Why can't you be honest with yourself? With me?" she finally demanded. "If you have something to say to me—just say it!"

"I have said it! But you don't want to accept it." Adam's face grew rocky. "The truth is I do feel responsible for you. I am concerned about you. You always seem to be leaving yourself wide open for pain and sorrow and that makes me want to protect you. Kelly, I just want to take care of you."

"I don't need a bodyguard!" Kelly cried. "What I need is a friend. That's what I thought you needed, too. If you want to be my friend, fine. If not, then just leave me alone."

Kelly tried to stop the last few words from spilling out of her mouth, but it was too late. Adam flinched, then his eyes went granite cold. Even though Kelly tried to find the words to apologize for her anger, the ride back to the office was an icy one.

11

A message from Jason was waiting for Kelly when she arrived at the office. He picked up on the first ring when she returned his call.

"Something's going down at the burned-out tenement tonight," Jason said without even returning her hello. "I just got an anonymous phone call saying I'd find some solid evidence to the arsonist inside the building. Can you meet me there at 9:00?"

"Jason, are you sure you're well enough to be crawling around an old building in this kind of weather?"

"Don't worry about me," he said. "Can you meet me or not? If not, I'll take my own pictures."

"No. I'll come. I just have to get clearance from the police first. Adam insisted." Kelly could hear Jason groan on the other end of the line.

"Oh. . .all right. Do what you have to do. Just be there." He hung up in her ear.

The police weren't as big an obstacle as Kelly feared. To be sure, they weren't particularly pleased with her request. They kept insisting they had searched the building thoroughly and had found nothing and that it was pointless for her to go poking around there again. But Kelly insisted it was her time to waste.

In the end, the police captain said he didn't give two hoots whether she went or not, but that he wasn't going to be held responsible for her if anything happened. Kelly told him that was fine with her and hung up.

At 8:30, Kelly donned parka and snowboots, grabbed a flashlight, and headed for the remains of the latest arson fire.

The scene was drearier than she'd anticipated. The old building was dingy and dirty inside and out. The entire first floor and half of the second were coated with ugly black soot. Someone had boarded up the front doors and windows, making entry through that part of the building impossible. Kelly's only other option was to return to the fire escape on the back side of the building and proceed from there.

Kelly waited over half an hour for Jason to show up, but there was no sign of him.

Had he gotten sick again, she wondered. She waited a few minutes more and was about to leave when she heard a thump coming from high up inside the building. She looked up just in time to see a flicker of light skitter past one of the windows on the third floor. *Maybe Jason found another way into the building and is waiting for me,* she thought.

For the second time, Kelly picked her way carefully up the rust-eaten stairway, testing each step tentatively before placing her full weight on it.

Arriving on the third story landing, just under the target window, she paused to reconnoiter. The window was shut. It hadn't been previously. In fact, Kelly recalled seeing a scrap of a curtain blowing around the rim the day she made her first climb.

Kelly placed her hand beneath the wooden crosspiece holding the pane in place and shoved upward as hard as she could, but the window wouldn't budge. Switching on her flashlight, she examined the window ledge and noticed large spikes nailed from the inside securing the window in place. Kelly ran the light back and forth within the room, but there was too much reflection off the glass to get a decent view.

Stepping back, Kelly glanced up at the fourth floor landing, shining the light up against the next window. Seeing no reflection, she switched off the light and proceeded up the stairs.

The climb was getting creepier by the minute. The blank, eyeless windows stared down at her from all angles. Kelly got the impression the building itself wore an expression of foreboding. The skeletal structure seemed to be warning her to go back, but she'd come too far to give up now.

Nervously, Kelly rounded the twist in the stairway and made her way to the next landing. This window was open. She entered easily.

She quickly made her way back down the inside steps to the third floor.

The room was all boarded up, but Kelly was able to pry the planks off with a stick she found laying in the hallway. It took a little effort, but she finally had the door open.

Unfortunately, her hard work didn't yield much of a result. The room was virtually empty except for an ancient, rat-eaten mattress, a decrepit old wardrobe with a cracked door, and a decrepit bureau with all but one drawer missing.

A mess of newspapers filled one corner, rat droppings another, and a pile of old tin cans were scattered on the mattress in the middle of the floor. It all looked pretty much like what one would expect to find in a condemned apartment building.

The only peculiar thing was the odor coming from the wardrobe—a smell Kelly would have described as something between kerosene and gasoline. She searched it thoroughly, but could find nothing producing the pungent odor.

Frustrated, Kelly returned to the pile of cans laying on the badly soiled mattress. Most were rusted through, although a couple of coffee cans looked newer. These had that same distinct odor, yet they were clean and dry.

Kelly poked around a little more, but found nothing that

seemed to help her investigation. Giving a little sigh of disappointment, Kelly scanned the room a couple more times with her flashlight. She was about to leave when her light caught the reflection of metal on top of the wardrobe.

She reached up over the top of her head to retrieve the shiny object. It was a small metal circlet, the size and shape of a woman's ring. She tried to grab hold of it, but it slid out from her hand and further back along the top of the wardrobe.

Kelly went to the corner of the room where the pile of old papers lay and grabbed a stack of them. She put them down in front of the wardrobe and climbed on top of them. They provided the added height she needed. But just as she was about to grasp the object, steely hands grabbed her around the waist.

She twisted in the stocky man's grip, then screamed as the flashlight fell to the floor. It was too dark, and the man was too close for Kelly to see his face, but she knew in that instant—it was Vince Rosselli.

Fear was replaced almost immediately with blatant anger. Kelly shoved and shoved hard, freeing herself momentarily from her captor. Vincent Rosselli's face was dark with fury as he turned on her.

"I warned you! I warned you to keep your mouth shut, but you wouldn't listen, would you?" His voice was low and menacing and thick with liquor.

Kelly managed to put the bureau between herself and the violent, embittered man. "What on earth are you talking about?"

"Why do you always insist on playing the innocent? You know perfectly well what I'm talking about! You told Edwards about that night, didn't you? Only you led him to believe it was all my fault! Well, I'm not going to be your scapegoat."

Vincent's voice dropped to a malignant murmur—hard and cold. "You told them to investigate my employment files, urged them to check the police records." He moved steadily toward her, but Kelly countered with her own evasive moves.

"You must have been very convincing in your theatrical

performance because he believed you. I'm sure you'll be pleased to learn that old man Edwards just told me I wouldn't become publisher of the *Chronicle.*"

Kelly gasped, but Vince was far too drunk to notice her reaction. His coal black eyes narrowed into bloodshot slits. "You've ruined me, Kelly. Because of one little mistake, I've lost everything."

"One little mistake! I hardly think your despicable, evil actions can be considered 'one little mistake'!"

"The only thing I ever did wrong was to love you."

"How can you call that love? It was an obsession! And because of that sick obsession, my father is dead! And you're responsible for that!"

"But I wasn't the one who killed him, was I?" Vincent's words shot through her like an arrow. "I wasn't the one driving the car, you were. You're the one to blame, not me!"

Kelly felt sick to her stomach. She slapped her hands over her ears, trying to blot out the terrible allegations Vincent flung at her, as well as the sickening sounds that echoed in her mind.

"How dare you try to unload your guilt on me! I'm the victim in this. Not you!" she screamed at him.

"And how dare you try to make me out a murderer! I never intended to hurt anyone, Kelly. It would never have happened if you hadn't tried to run away from me."

"What should I have done, Vincent? Let you hurt me? You were drunk, just like you are right now. And you were irrational, just like right now. You wouldn't listen to reason. You didn't want to hear the truth. . .that I didn't love you. . .and could never love you."

"You led me on. You made me believe you cared about me. I had great plans for you, Kelly, but you just tossed me aside."

"I never led you to believe anything about us. They were fantasies you made up in your own mind. I told you from the start that I could never get involved with you."

"Oh, sure! Can't get involved with the boss, right? You seem to have changed your tune about that, now, haven't you?" he said accusingly.

Kelly recoiled at his cutting truth. Her heart was hammering against her ribcage. "It's more than that. When I first started working for you, I respected and trusted you. But you destroyed all of that."

"And you used me," he shot back. "You took everything I offered and gave me nothing but pious preaching in return. You talked of love all the time, but they were hollow words. When I asked you to love me, I got nothing but a slap in the face."

"I talked of God's love, not romantic love. You chose to twist the meaning of the words."

"I loved you, Kelly. I still do. We could be so good together. If you would just relax a little bit. If you wouldn't be so prudish ...so judgmental. It's not too late. I can still feel the electricity between us."

Revulsion shocked Kelly. She had to turn his thoughts away from her—from the two of them together. *Lord, please help me!* The desperate prayer sprang from her heart.

"What about Whitney?"

"What about her?"

"Don't you care about her at all?"

Vincent squinted at her. "Whitney has proven very useful to me. And I to her. Together, we've made a good team. But the bottom line is that she wants Adam. And I want you!"

Kelly shuddered at the look in his eye. "Vincent, there's an evil eating away inside you. You're sick and drunk. How could you ever believe I'd have anything to do with you? Why don't you just leave town, now? You don't have to stay here."

"Sorry to disappoint you, Kelly, but I'm not leaving. You've taken the only thing I've ever wanted in my life away from me: my work. Not once, but twice. I can't just leave it at that."

His voice had taken on a new malevolence, but the words were delivered with an evenness to them as if he were explaining a mathematical problem.

"You see, when you take something away from me, I must take something away from you. . .to balance things out, so to speak. And it must be something of great value. That is the price you must pay for telling secrets." He lurched at her, grabbing for her arm but missing.

"I haven't told anyone, anything!" Kelly jumped away. "I never wanted to destroy you—even though you deserve to be ruined!"

"Art thou now my judge, Saint Kelly?" The cruel, sardonic smile was back on his face, taunting her, humiliating her, cutting through her layers of defense with incredible precision. Vincent Rosselli had always known exactly the right slices to take to wound her where it hurt most.

"Judge not, lest thou be judged, my little hypocrite."

Fury and outrage boiled in Kelly's heart as Vincent lunged for her. This time he caught her shoulders, pinning her against the old wardrobe.

The doorknob cut deep into her back. The smell of his foul, liquor-laden breath nauseated her. For a brief instant she was back in Detroit, in a steamy parking lot on a hot August night. The hard chrome of a car door handle knifing her in the back as she struggled with this same evil creature. That night, it had been intense fear that had driven Kelly blindly along. Tonight, it was pure, unadulterated hatred.

"Let go of me, you slimy viper! Let go of me or I'll . . .I'll. . ."

"Or you'll what? Call on your God to send down His lightning bolt and strike me dead? Well, go ahead! Do it! Do it!" He shook her as he laughed in her face.

"Where is your God now, Kelly? Is he going to come rescue you?" He placed his right hand around her throat. "Or is he going to punish you for your hypocrisy by letting Satan squeeze the life right out of you?"

Fear overtook her, paralyzing her. The blood drained from

Kelly's face as the cold, clammy hand tightened about her throat.

"That *is* what you think, isn't it, Kelly? That I'm the devil himself. Don't you know you should never pick a fight with the devil?" His face was but a few inches from her own. He read the fear in her eyes and squeezed harder.

"Let. . .go. . .of. . .me!" she repeated through clenched teeth, her voice hoarse from the pressure being applied on her larynx.

"Not until you admit your guilt. Say it, Kelly! Tell me it was you who told John Edwards about the accident! Why deny it? You wanted to see me destroyed. Admit it, Kelly! It was you who ruined any chance I ever had of making it in this town, just like you ruined my chances in Detroit."

He tightened his grip yet again and Kelly began to black out. She clawed frantically with her free hand at the one that held her neck, but she had already used up too much of her energy fighting for air. In a last ditch attempt, she kicked out at him, but suddenly found herself striking out into thin air. It was a second or two before she realized the vise-like grip on her throat was gone.

As her head started to clear, Kelly could see Vincent now backed up against the wardrobe, his face red and swollen with rage, his own throat caught in a steely grip. The hand that held him was strong and powerful, the fingers taut and sinewy. Her eyes traveled up the arm and shoulder and came to rest on ice-gray eyes.

"The lady told you to let go of her," Adam said, his tone murderously flat. "Perhaps you can't hear very well."

Vincent swung out at him with both fists, but Adam easily deflected the blows. He adjusted his grip on the pudgy neck, and Vincent's face went white.

Dear God, Kelly thought, *he's going to kill him.*

For a brief instant, a flash of utter shame washed through Kelly as she realized she didn't find that idea so distasteful. But, finally, she found her voice.

"Adam, don't! Don't hurt him! He's not worth it!"

Adam glanced at her, hesitated, then looked at Vince as if seeing him for the first time.

"She's right, you know," Adam said, more to himself than Vince. "You are the most pitiful, wretched creature I've ever seen." He took in a long deep breath and let it out slowly.

"A minute ago, I could have squashed you like an insect and never thought twice about it. But now I see there's nothing but emptiness in you. I don't know how you can stand it…being so alone and miserable and frightened. It must make you feel like the most insignificant, useless worm on the face of the earth."

A new expression settled in Adam's eyes. He relaxed his grip and stepped back.

Vincent took the opportunity to tackle him, but Adam easily sidestepped him, and Vincent went sprawling on his own drunken accord. He picked himself up and whirled around to charge again when a sound at the door snapped them toward it.

"Just what the blazes are all of you doing here?!" George McClanahan shone a flashlight directly in Kelly's eyes.

"We might ask you the same thing, Inspector," Adam responded, the first to regain his composure.

"It's my job to check out this building. But you—you have no authority to be in here. I don't want to hear any of your excuses. I'll give you three minutes to get out, or I'll place you under arrest. Got it?"

Adam grabbed Kelly's arm and guided her through the lower levels of the burned out building, helping her through the front entrance where he'd forced one of the planks out of the way.

When they were alone, Kelly collapsed in Adam's arms, the emotional turmoil of the night finally catching up with her.

"Are you all right, Kelly?" Adam cradled her sobbing form tightly in his arms. "Let me see if he hurt you." He coaxed her hands away from her face and inspected the marks on her neck. "You'll probably have a few bruises there tomorrow," he said, as he gently stroked her chin and cheek. "Come on, let's get you home." He bundled her up and helped her out to his car.

Adam didn't say anything to Kelly as they drove home. She was numb with shock and wouldn't have been able to respond coherently anyway. It wasn't until she was safe in her own apartment that she finally found her voice.

"I was wrong, Adam."

He looked at her, puzzled.

"I guess I do need a bodyguard."

Adam's wry smile in response to her declaration eased the tension in the room.

"Then, I guess you'll forgive me for checking up on you."

"How did you know I'd be there?"

"Jason called a little while ago. He said he'd checked out his informant's story and couldn't verify any of it, so he figured it was just a crank. When Jason couldn't get hold of you, he called me. I suspect our 'informant' was Vincent trying to get you alone. I just thank God I was able to get there in time."

Kelly smiled shakily at him and said she'd been thanking God, too.

"You know, *I* was wrong," Adam continued. "I *do* care a great deal about you. I admitted that to myself tonight. When I saw you with Vince, I wasn't only afraid for your safety, I was completely overcome with jealousy. I know that sounds awful, but I wanted to tear him apart."

"You could have done it, too, couldn't you?"

"Yes. I suppose, with my Marine Corps training, I could have done him a lot of damage." His gray eyes probed her cocoa-colored ones.

"Why didn't you?" she asked, her eyebrow cocked in its naturally quizzical position.

"I suppose because I suddenly pitied him. I heard him profess his love for you, and I remembered what you said about people getting all twisted up in their thinking when it comes to love. He just seemed so pathetic—and I just felt sorry for him."

"You felt sorry for him?" Kelly asked incredulously. "After

102

he tried to kill me?"

"You almost sound like you're sorry I didn't hurt him," Adam replied. "Surely you wouldn't have wanted me to do that. You're the one who made me stop."

His statement made her pause. "Of course not," Kelly finally replied, but there wasn't much conviction in her statement.

"Then why do you seem so upset that I showed the man a little compassion?"

A knot of anger formed in Kelly's throat, and it made her even angrier to realize she didn't know where the emotion was coming from.

"Maybe I'm upset because the man just tried to kill me and you seem to be defending him." Kelly clamped her jaw and gritted her teeth.

"But, I was right there," Adam offered. "I would never have let him hurt you." He went to put his arm around her but she brushed him off.

"Just how long *were* you there?" she demanded. "How much did you hear?"

"Enough to know he feels quite deeply about you. I know his thinking is all warped, but you said such a person needs to be treated with compassion and understanding."

"I wasn't speaking about Vince Rosselli at the time. The man is pure evil. He doesn't deserve anyone's mercy."

"He's still a human being, though," Adam challenged. "With all the flaws and fallibilities that implies. He's hurting, Kelly. The man is at the bottom of the pit."

"And that gives him the right to attack me?" Kelly's voice had risen a half-step.

"Of course not." Adam lowered his voice. "Just like my jealousy gave me no right to attack him. I'm just trying to understand what happened between the two of you that would cause you to be so irrational when it comes to him."

"I'm irrational? He tries to kill me and *I'm* irrational?" Her voice raised two more steps to an almost uncontrollable pitch.

Adam grabbed her by the shoulders. "Kelly, stop it! Look at you! Look what you're letting him do to you. It's all over with, and you still look like you could murder him. When I look at you now, at the rage you're in, I have to wonder if Rosselli wasn't right. Maybe you did do something to try to get back at him."

"You don't know anything!" she lashed out at him. "Whatever happened to Rosselli was his own doing. Call it poetic justice."

"I know enough to be able to tell the difference between justice and revenge. And right now the only thing I see in you is revenge."

Kelly's brown eyes grew black, her nostrils flared, and Adam could see the hollows of her cheeks work as she ground her teeth.

"You don't know what he did to me! You don't know what he cost me!"

"No, I don't, but you told me it didn't matter what anyone did to you, that being angry wouldn't change anything. You said it's necessary to forgive others as God forgives us. Didn't you mean what you said, Kelly? Or doesn't it apply to you?"

Kelly turned her head, refusing to answer him.

"You said we can learn to forgive anything. Was that a lie?" When there was still no response, Adam lowered his eyes and shook his head.

"Perhaps Whitney and Rosselli were right all along. Maybe you are a hypocrite."

At his last remark, something snapped in Kelly's brain. In horror she watched as her hand sprung out to strike Adam across the face.

Kelly stared at the hand as if it wasn't a part of her own body. She was shaking uncontrollably. Adam gazed at her in shocked silence for several seconds, then turned abruptly and walked out of the apartment.

Kelly grabbed the arm of the chair to steady herself, but now even that couldn't support her weight. Slowly she sank to her knees in the middle of the thick, braided carpet. She didn't even realize she was crying until she felt the large, wet drops plunk onto her blouse.

"Oh Father, what have I done?" she cried out in a hoarse whisper. Her mind, like an overloaded electrical panel, suddenly short-circuited and went numb. The tears became a waterfall and her body writhed with the aching sobs, but her mind could no longer comprehend the pain.

She doubled over in agony, growing smaller and smaller as she laid out her soul before the Lord. She was shaking with cries of deepest despair.

"Lord, I am a hypocrite. . . .Father, forgive me. . .Lord, mercy, please, Lord. . . ."

12

Kelly had no idea how long she lay on the floor. It seemed like hours before she was able to function on even the most basic of levels. She slowly gathered herself together, her emotions spent, her body numb. She pulled herself up into the arms of the over-stuffed recliner in the corner of the room, grabbed a box of tissues from the shelf behind her, wiped her eyes and nose, and dabbed at the tearstains spotting her slacks.

Gradually, the novocaine of the shock wore off. She knew she needed to pray and made several attempts to form words to express herself, but she could not.

Picking up her Bible, she turned to a favorite passage in Romans: "...For we do not know how to pray as we should, but the Spirit Himself intercedes for us with groanings too deep for words; and He who searches the hearts knows what the mind of the Spirit is, because He intercedes for the saints according to the will of God."

For several minutes, Kelly made no noise or movement, begging the Lord to hear the very groanings of her heart instead. When she finally did speak, it was to make one petition—for God to show her the truth about Adam's accusations.

His answer was immediately clear and made her redden with

shame. God had spoken to her heart. She knew what she needed to do. Now all she needed was the courage. She got up slowly, went to the bathroom, and splashed cold water on her face. When she felt somewhat revived, she straightened her hair and clothes, threw on her coat, and went out the door. Kelly hailed a cab and picked up her car.

Cold determination drove her through the night. A sense of rightness pushed her up the steps of the front entrance of the apartment complex and through the doors of the elevator. But it wasn't until she came face to face with his doorbell, that she hesitated. At that moment she realized how late the hour was, or should she say early, since it had to be at least 2 or 3 o'clock in the morning.

She was about to turn back, but knew if she didn't do it now, she wouldn't do it at all. Resolutely, she pressed the buzzer and waited. And waited. And waited. Her courage draining away, little by little. Finally, she rapped lightly and called out Adam's name.

"Go away!" came the stiff reply.

"Adam, please," Kelly pleaded with him softly. "I have to talk with you."

"Well, I don't want to talk with you. There's nothing you can say that will excuse your actions tonight. I think for the first time since I've known you, I've seen the real Kelly Jordan."

"Adam, please, let me in," Kelly persisted. "I need to apologize to you."

"That's your problem."

The coldness in his voice couldn't have hurt her more if he had returned her slap across the face. It suddenly became imperative that she explain things to Adam. No matter what the cost to her pride.

"Adam, I'm not leaving until you let me in. I know I deserve nothing from you. But you *do* deserve an apology from me. You don't have to accept it. It's yours to do with as you like. But, please let me make it in person and not through a closed door."

There was a long moment of silence, then she heard the deadbolt slide back. Her heart pounded at the sound. She pulled herself up, steeling herself for whatever was to come.

He stood before her, barefoot and muffled in a thick black wraparound bathrobe over his clothes. His hair was rumpled, his eyes gaunt and weary, but they weren't as icy as his voice.

"Make it quick," he said curtly. "It's late, and I've already wasted too much time on you."

She stepped inside the apartment without an invitation, leaving the door open behind her. He didn't offer her a seat, so she leaned against the doorframe, suddenly weak from emotion. She held her hands behind her back and bowed her head. She could no longer meet the cold gray eyes.

In the endless moment that followed, she gathered her thoughts and courage. When she spoke, it was in a trembling whisper.

"Everything you said about me tonight was the truth. That's why it hurt so much."

She waited for him to say something. When he did not, she continued, haltingly. "For two years now, I've been pretending I'm a good Christian—compassionate, caring—yet all the time I've harbored hatred in my heart.

"Deep down inside, I knew the resentment was there, but I didn't want to acknowledge it because it would mean I'd have to forgive Vincent for his part in the death of my father. And frankly, I–I didn't feel like he'd been punished enough for the pain he caused me. I conveniently forgot it's not my place to punish. The Lord pointed that out to me tonight. . .rather painfully."

She paused again and was met with more silence.

"Adam, when you used my own words to show me how spiteful and malicious I was being, it drove home the truth. I suddenly saw myself in a whole new light. . .and it wasn't a pretty picture. I was—am—ashamed of myself, and of the lie I've been living.

"When you called me a hypocrite, I knew you were right, and I couldn't handle it. I was also very angry—angry at myself, at God, at Vincent. I took that anger out on you and for that I'm deeply sorry. I don't expect you to forgive me, but you need to know my actions tonight were my own doing. *I* am solely responsible for them, not Vincent, or you, or God—just me."

There was still no response, and Kelly became truly alarmed that the damage she had done was irreparable.

"I've made my confession to God, and I know He's forgiven me, but it's imperative that I do whatever I can to make amends to you for my behavior. That's why I'm here now."

Adam cocked his head, set his jaw and squinted, scrutinizing her with uncertain silver eyes. "And I'm supposed to forgive you, too? Just like that."

"No," she said in a shaky whisper. "After my miserable display of unforgiveness, I have no right to expect anyone to forgive me at the drop of an apology. I was wrong, Adam. You were right."

A tear she'd been struggling to keep from slipping down her cheek finally got its own way.

"It's not as easy as I thought for human beings to forgive. It's not easy at all. Only God can forgive that way."

"You're still convinced of that?" There was no sarcasm in Adam's voice. "If *we* can't forgive others of little sins, how can *God* forgive us of big ones?"

"Because He's God. . .He loves us. . .He isn't like you and me," she replied.

"But why? Why does God love us?"

His questions disturbed Kelly. Was she being put through some kind of test, she wondered. She answered carefully, thoughtfully.

"Because He created us and, having created us. . .having loved us freely. . .He is willing to do whatever is necessary to keep us close to Him."

"But we keep right on sinning," Adam persisted. "Why

would Jesus die for people who keep hurting Him?"

Kelly was becoming increasingly distressed by his line of questioning. She tried to answer as best she could but knew the words were inadequate. "Because He understands us. He's been here before...faced the same temptations...known the same sorrows. A wise man once said: 'To understand *everything* is to be able to forgive *anything*.'

"Jesus knows everything about you...about me. He knows why I did what I did, why I think like I think, why I am like I am. He knows everything that's ever happened to me and how it's affected my life. He understands how hard it is to be a human being because He was one—and, understanding *everything*, He offers His unlimited forgiveness and unconditional love to every one of us, without hesitation."

Adam's face softened as he listened to her. A light flickered, then came to life in the penetrating eyes. He reached for her arm and guided her into the living room. He seated her on the blue and cream-colored couch, then chose a matching chair directly across from her.

"I want to believe you. And I want to be able to forgive," he said. "But you'll have to help me."

"I don't know what more I can say, Adam."

"Maybe if *I* understood what was going on tonight, I'd be able to believe and forgive, too. Kelly, tell me what happened between you and Vince."

She hadn't expected that. But after saying what she just did, she had no choice. She took a long, shaky breath, bracing herself for the raw emotions she knew would surely surface in the retelling of the tragic events.

"All right," she said quietly, "I'll tell you.

"I met Vincent while working for the *Detroit Gazette*. I was fresh out of college, had never held a full time job before, and was eager to start my career out on the right foot.

"I was still living at home at the time, trying to save money to pay off debts from my college education.

"When I found out I'd been hired by the *Gazette*, I was ecstatic! Even more thrilling was finding out I'd be working with one of the top journalism teams right off the bat. I realize now Rosselli had a lot to do with that—pulling strings at higher levels—but I didn't know it then.

"You're going to think I'm pretty stupid, but I really believed he just wanted to give a young reporter a break. I didn't know he had anything else in mind until months later.

"At first, Vince treated me more like a sister than anything else—always looking out for me, even to the point of warning me about what places to stay out of and which guys to watch out for. But after a couple of months, I noticed some subtle changes in his behavior.

"It began with a few simple compliments about my looks or clothes, but then the comments became innuendos, and finally, outright propositions.

"I guess I was kind of dumb at the time, because I assumed he was joking, and I joked right back. Not only was it wrong, it was the worst thing I could have done because it just fueled his fantasies. It didn't take long after that for things to get out of hand. Vince began hanging around me a lot which made me extremely uncomfortable. It got worse and worse until one night we finally had it out."

Kelly's voice drifted off for a few seconds as the memories came flooding back.

"We'd been working late. It was a hot summer night. The air-conditioning at the paper had been on the fritz and most everyone had gone home early to try and cool off. Vince and I were alone putting the paper to bed when he came over and invited me to dinner. He wouldn't take 'no' for an answer. He insisted on driving and took me to a supper club on the outskirts of the city.

"I should have known something was up because Vince was acting stranger than usual. He drank a lot at dinner. I got scared and asked him if he didn't think he'd had enough.

111

"That only made him angry. I remember he reached out and grabbed me by the arm. He told me I should 'just relax' and enjoy his company.

"He became obnoxious and overbearing, not just with me but also with everyone around us. He was annoying the waitresses, making crude remarks and leering at them. I was really embarrassed.

"Finally, I told him I wasn't feeling well and wanted to go home. When I got up to leave, he grabbed me and pulled me back down in the chair. By this time, I was frantic.

"He had a couple more drinks while I sat there, waiting. Then one of his buddies came over to the table and I saw my chance to leave.

"While they were talking, I excused myself to go to the ladies room, but I kept right on walking out the door. I hailed a cab and headed back to the paper to get my car. It was quite late by this time, and I hadn't remembered to call my folks to let them know where I was going or when I would be home. I knew they'd be worried. What I didn't know was that my dad would come looking for me. . ." Kelly's voice broke.

"I'm sorry," she said as she struggled to regain her composure. "I thought I had worked through all this before, but I see I have a long way to go."

"It's okay," Adam said gently. "I shouldn't have made you tell me. You don't have to go on if you don't want to."

"No. No. . .I need to tell you. Maybe it will help me understand it all myself." She took a deep breath, swallowed hard and continued.

"I don't know how he did it—how Vince beat me back to the office. He must have figured out what I'd done almost immediately.

"I saw him drive up as I was paying off the cabby. I made a mad dash for the car, but, as usual, I'd locked all the doors and had to fumble around in my purse to find the key. I had just unlocked the door when he caught me and pinned me against

112

the car. He was saying awful things, accusing me of being a tease, yelling at me to stop acting like a little girl. It was horrible.

"I tried to push him away, but he kept telling me what I needed was a real man in my life. He tried to kiss me, and I slapped him across the face. But that didn't stop him. It only made him angrier.

"I think he really would have hurt me except a car drove into the parking lot just then. It distracted him long enough for me to break away from him and get inside my car. I locked the door and started the engine. Vince was standing there pounding on the door, swearing at me. . . .I wasn't thinking too clearly, I just wanted to get away. I put the car into gear and gunned the engine. I never even looked. . . ." Her voice broke again and tears trickled down her cheeks.

"It was your father," Adam finished softly. Kelly shook her head numbly.

"He had called the office when it had gotten so late. One of the night guys told him I wasn't there, but that my car was still in the lot.

"Daddy got worried and decided he'd just drive around to make sure I was all right. He saw me struggling with Vince, had gotten out of the car to help me, but by that time I was already making my escape.

"I never saw him standing there. I just heard that awful thud . . .the sound of the windshield cracking. . . .He never regained consciousness. I never even had a chance to tell him I was sorry." Kelly choked on the final words and couldn't continue.

Long minutes of silence followed, and Kelly cried silent sobs of agony. Adam's face was filled with pained sympathy, but he made no move to go to her.

"It was an accident," he said, at last. "You obviously loved your father very much. He had to know that, too.

"He wouldn't have wanted you to condemn yourself for what happened. You made a mistake. I know it was a costly one, but every one of us makes mistakes from time to time, some just as costly as the one you made." Grief swept Adam's face, then was quickly replaced with a steely gaze.

"Take Rosselli for example. He's just as much to blame for what happened as anyone else."

"Maybe," Kelly acknowledged, "but that doesn't change the fact that I was the one behind the wheel that night. Yes, my actions were a direct result of Vincent's behavior. But the truth is, Vince paid for his part in the whole thing. I didn't. He was arrested for drunk and disorderly conduct and assault.

"I'm a Christian, Adam, I should never have given in to Vince, never gone out with him. I knew he wasn't a Christian. Then. . .after everything was over. . .I shouldn't have felt the need for any further revenge on him, but the hatred was still there.

"I filed a harassment complaint against him with the company. That's when they fired him. And even that wasn't enough for me. I still harbored the hurt.

"In a way, it might have been easier on me if *I* had been punished. Maybe then I could have closed the door on the whole episode. But the way it is now, I can never forget what happened that night. I killed my father." Kelly's voice was a raw, anguished whisper. "The knowledge that I'm responsible for taking the life of another human being—someone I loved so much—is something that will haunt me for as long as I live. Daddy didn't deserve to die. He was only there to help me."

At her final words, Adam stood, his face ashen, his eyes nondescript liquid paleness. An expression of indescribable emptiness swept his face.

Kelly glanced up, furtively searching the granite face, then panicked as he turned his back on her. The rejection of that instant was almost overwhelming, and she struggled to fight back a fresh thrust of piercing pain.

Adam moved toward the stone fireplace in the corner of the living room. He gripped the mantle with both hands, his back rigid and straight.

Tears strangled Kelly's speech, but she managed to force the words out anyway. "I know I've been a really poor example of a Christian. That's what I regret more than anything else. My actions have hurt a lot of people, including you, and that's something I never, ever wanted to do. I wish I could take back all the pain I've caused you, but I can't."

Kelly's eyes fixed on the back of the silent form standing a few feet from her. It was a struggle to go on, but she forced herself to finish what she'd started.

"I can, however, make sure no one else suffers from this. I'm going to apologize to Vincent. And there is the strong possibility that he will go public with the whole thing. I'm perfectly aware how this could affect the credibility of the *Journal* and I'll understand if you want me to resign. I certainly don't want to be an embarrassment to you or the paper."

Adam remained tensed and silent as if grappling for control and comprehension.

"Like I said before, I don't expect your forgiveness—but I do hope someday you'll be able to understand." She waited for him to respond, but he said nothing.

She rose and stood, staring at his back, uncertain if she should go or stay. What this particular person thought of her did matter to her. It mattered a great deal. Just when she had decided to leave, he turned toward her, and she was shocked to see tears in his eyes.

"Understand?" he said. "I not only understand, I've been there."

13

Despite the tears, Adam's voice was expressionless, his tone, composed and devoid of inflection. He wiped the wetness from his eyes with the heel of his hand and took a shaky breath.

"Do you remember that night after the Bible study when we talked about Helen's death?"

Kelly nodded.

"Do you remember I told you how responsible I felt for her death?"

Kelly nodded again.

"I meant that literally. If it hadn't been for me, Helen might be alive right now."

"But the fire wasn't your fault!" Kelly protested.

"No," Adam replied. "But Helen wouldn't have been at the house that night if I hadn't ordered her to stay home."

He turned away from her again, returning to the fireplace where random tongues of flame licked at a white birch log. He grasped the mantle with white-knuckled fingers and stood staring into the glowing embers.

Kelly took a step closer to him, studying the profile of pain. The scar along his jaw line stood out in the dim light. She wanted to reach out to him, but the look of suffering stiffening his body stopped her.

Adam was obviously battling to master his emotions. He had them under a tight rein for the moment, but Kelly sensed that it wouldn't take much to unleash them. She remained silent, and in a second, he continued.

"Helen was a lot like you," he said. "Alive and exciting and giving one hundred percent of herself in everything she did...." His eyes glistened with the memory as he turned to face her.

"Did you know she was a reporter for the paper?"

"No," Kelly answered softly.

"Well, she was. The best! Maybe she was too good. She was aggressive, always taking chances, just like you. I worried about her all the time. I was always afraid she would get hurt covering a dangerous assignment." He paused, then said, "It's almost ironic that she died the way she did. You see, it was for that very reason I made her stay home the night of the fire." Adam glanced at Kelly.

"Helen was pregnant." Again, the matter-of-fact tone masked his pain. "We had known about it for a few months and were overjoyed. We'd been waiting three years for that moment. That's why I didn't want her taking any chances.

"The night of the fire, Jason called in a report of a hostage situation happening in the inner city.

"He wanted to go himself, but I didn't think he was quite mature enough to handle something so big. Normally, I would have assigned Helen to the story since she was my senior reporter, but because of the baby, I decided to go myself.

"Helen was furious. She took it as a personal criticism. I didn't intend it as such. It's just that there had been reports of gunshots, and I didn't want anything to happen to her or the baby. Helen said she trusted the Lord to watch out for her, why couldn't I?

"There wasn't time to argue, so I put my foot down and insisted she stay home. I knew she wasn't happy about it, but I knew she wouldn't defy me, either.

"A few hours later, the hostage situation was resolved, and I headed back to the office to write up the article while it was still fresh in my mind. I should have gone home." For the first time that night Adam's voice wavered.

"I should have—but I didn't. By the time I finally arrived, the garage was in flames. Someone had already called the fire department, but there was so much smoke in the house they were having trouble locating Helen. I figured she must be in the bedroom and went in to get her. Part of the roof collapsed as I struggled to get her out, that's when this happened." He ran a forefinger along the scar.

"We were too late." Weariness, in addition to sadness, crept into his voice. Heaviness clung to his words.

"She'd stopped breathing. They didn't know for how long. They were able to resuscitate her, and we took her to the hospital, but she never came out of the coma. There was always the hope in the back of my mind that maybe we could save the baby. But complications set in the third week after the fire and then Helen developed pneumonia.

"We eventually lost the child. Soon afterward, the doctors told me I had to decide whether or not to take Helen off life support.

"I remember how angry I was at God at that moment. I kept thinking He couldn't possibly mean to take them both from me. At first, I believed God would perform some kind of miracle and give Helen back to me. I knew He could. But sitting with her day after day, I realized that was never going to happen.

"Most of that time in the hospital is just a blur now. I don't remember much, just the sounds of the respirator and the heart monitor and the smell of disinfectant. . . ."

Kelly could see the strain Adam was under as he related the story. She studied his gaunt eyes. . .noticed the pain etched in every line of his face. She made a move to stop him from going on with the tale, but he held up a restraining hand and insisted on finishing the account.

"That last day, I had gone down to the chapel. I guess I was hoping God would give me a sign. Let me know what I should do. While I was there, I held my own private memorial service for the baby.

"Until then, losing the child hadn't seemed real to me. But as I knelt and prayed, I began to feel the loss for the first time. It was painful, but it was also a relief to be able to acknowledge my feelings. Not many people knew about Helen's pregnancy. And those that did didn't seem to think it should matter so much. After all, they said, I really didn't have a chance to know the baby. . . ."

Adam was quiet for a few seconds, then added, "You know—even when people found out about the child, no one ever bothered to ask if it was a boy or a girl."

Silence engulfed them. Kelly placed her hand on his shoulder but couldn't speak.

"It was a girl," he finally said.

"It was then that I realized what I had to do. My daughter was dead but at least I knew she was in heaven. But Helen?. . .She was caught somewhere between life and death.

"That's when I finally made the decision. I talked to the doctors; I called in consultants. They all said the same thing: There was no brain activity. The machine was breathing for her. There was no chance for recovery. I lost count of the number of doctors who told me that. Then, her vital organs began shutting down. Her kidneys failed. Finally, I had to let them disconnect the respirator. So I notified the doctors and signed all the papers and then sat and held Helen's hand as she took her last breath."

Adam swallowed hard. "Two innocent lives lost, and I'm the one to blame for it all. Do I know what it's like to be responsible for taking the life of another person? Yes, I guess I do."

"You made the only decision you could." It was Kelly's turn to comfort. "You did what you felt was right."

"That's not the point," he responded. "I should have trusted

119

Helen and let her take the newspaper assignment. She trusted me. . .and I betrayed that trust.

"Because of my stubbornness, I put both her and the baby in jeopardy. And in the end, I denied Helen a last chance at life."

"No," Kelly said gently, but firmly. "In the end, you let go of her and let God give her *new* life. And that, my friend, is the most selfless thing anyone could have done.

"We've both made mistakes, Adam. There's no denying that, but they aren't unforgivable mistakes. No matter how bad they seem, God can pardon us and free us from all the guilt.

"Just look at us, Adam. Look what we've done to ourselves. We've forgotten the most important thing Christians can forget—forgiveness. God's forgiveness—waiting for us if we'll only ask. God has already forgiven us—in entirety, for eternity—and we need to do likewise. Then maybe we can let go of the past."

Adam turned toward her. "Pray with me," he said softly.

She took his hand, and they knelt together beside the fire and prayed for God's grace and forgiveness. As the burden of guilt and sin lifted from their hearts, they both began to weep. But the tears they cried were not of despair and pain. They wept tears of repentance, and pardon, and reconciliation.

As Kelly talked with her heavenly Father, she felt relief flood through her. To her, it seemed as if someone had turned on a faucet and washed away all the pain and the hurt and the dirt that had accumulated over the past two years.

When Kelly finally pulled away, her eyes were wet, her nose was running, and she desperately needed a tissue. Adam finally produced one from a nearby box, keeping one for himself. She smiled up at him and said something about looking a mess, but he just smiled back and brushed the hair away from her face.

Adam held out a hand to help Kelly to her feet. "I'm not really sure where we're supposed to go from from here," he said. "You've turned my life upside down. You've made me want to love again and that scares me. You know, everything was so much simpler before you came along."

"And so much more lonely," she added reflectively.

"And indescribably lonely," he agreed.

He gazed into her eyes for a moment, then pulled her into his arms and simply held her for a long, long time.

When he released her, she pulled her coat tighter around her and fairly floated toward the door. Adam walked with her, a protective arm wrapped around her.

As they lingered in the doorway, Adam reached out to take her hand, then pressed the delicate fingers to his lips. Kelly became acutely aware of a pervasive tingling sensation that started at the point where his lips met her hand and coursed its way up along her arm. She let the warmth trickle down into her soul like the patter of summer rain.

"I have to go," she said, as much to herself as to Adam. "It's late."

Adam nodded.

As Kelly walked to the elevator, Adam turned back to his apartment. Kelly called out good-night to him then stepped into the elevator. As the door slid silently closed behind her, Adam entered his own apartment. Neither one of them saw the figure that had watched the entire scene from the dark shadows of the hallway.

14

"Out kind of late, aren't you?"

Kelly spun around, dropping the key she'd been fumbling with as she tried to unlock her apartment door.

"Whitney! What on earth are you doing here? You nearly scared me to death sneaking up on me like that!"

"Looks like I'm not the only one sneaking around tonight," she said pointedly. Whitney's green eyes wore a cat-that-swallowed-the-canary grin that gave Kelly the shivers.

Kelly retrieved her keys and opened the door.

"Aren't you going to ask me in?" Whitney maneuvered herself into the middle of the doorway, then skirted around Kelly.

"That seems to be a rhetorical question since you already *are* in." Kelly eyed her uninvited guest with growing annoyance.

"Excuse me if I don't offer you a seat, but I know you can't stay." Kelly threw her keys and purse on the kitchen counter. "Now then, I know this can't be a social visit, so why don't you just tell me what you're doing here."

"Well, at least you're direct, Jordan. I'll give you that."

Kelly ignored the remark. She walked back to the door, opened it and gestured for Whitney to leave.

"Either tell me what you want or leave now."

Instead of following Kelly, Whitney turned and perched herself on the edge of the sofa, resuming her cocky smile.

"Temper, temper!" She clicked her tongue. "My, how we do get owly when we've been out all night." She stretched her svelte form on the couch, making herself completely at home. "Relax, Kelly. I've come to do you a favor. I've come to give you some friendly advice."

"About what? How to cause trouble?"

"Actually, it's about how to save your reputation. . .and Adam's."

Kelly's eyebrow shot up. "Why would you care about my reputation?"

"I don't care about yours," Whitney retorted. "I *do* care about Adam's. And his isn't going to look very good if the news gets out that you've been spending your nights at his place."

"And what makes you think that's where I've been spending my time?"

"I don't think. I know." Whitney replied with smug confidence. "In fact, I've found out quite a lot about the two of you tonight. For instance, I know you, Vince, and Adam were poking around that burned-out building this evening. I know Adam took you home, that you had a fight, and that he left here in a huff.

"I also know you followed him to his apartment. In fact, you've just come from there."

"How could you know all that?"

"Why, Kelly, I *am* an investigative reporter. I have my sources."

"You mean you've been spying on us!" Kelly was outraged by her audacity.

"Well, someone has to look out for Adam now that you've got your hooks into him. He sure isn't using any common sense. All it would take is just a few details of your little rendezvous to get out and the rumors would start flying."

"And I'm sure you'd be more than happy to see that happen!" Kelly gave the dark-haired woman a scathing glance.

"Actually. . .no. You see, I really do care about Adam. And, unlike you, I want to see him stay out of trouble—not drag him into it."

"Well, then you can just relax, because I'm not 'involved' with Adam. At least, not the way you think."

"But that's not the way it *looks*, Jordan. And looks can be easily misinterpreted."

"Even so, what you're suggesting is hardly scandalous in this day and age. No one's going to care if I'm seeing my boss."

The catty smirk returned to Whitney's lips. "You're right. That isn't much of a bulletin. But, how's this for an attention getter: EXTRA! EXTRA! READ ALL ABOUT IT! STAR PHOTOJOURNALIST RUNS DOWN OWN FATHER!" Whitney set the invisible words in the air in front of her as she read them off. Then she turned her fiery emerald eyes back on Kelly.

Kelly's heart sank to the pit of her stomach. She had the distinct impression Whitney was drawing her into a trap—and that Whitney held the trip switch. Kelly tried to remain cool and unruffled.

"So—you know. I guess I shouldn't be surprised."

Kelly took a deep breath, studying her opponent. What she said next would be critical to the outcome of Whitney's little game. Kelly tread carefully.

"The only trouble with trying to use that information against me is that it's already part of the public record. And that record also shows I was exonerated of all charges in the death of my father. What's more, Adam already knows the truth about the whole thing and it doesn't matter to him."

"Your guilt or innocence—or even what Adam thinks—isn't the issue here," Whitney retaliated. "It's what your past could do to Adam. Think, you silly little twit. Just think what will happen if the press finds out that one of Bingham's leading citizens—the editor of one of the most prestigious papers in the state—is involved with a woman who ran down and killed her own father!

"Do you honestly believe they're going to stop there? No! Once those reporters get hold of this information, they'll turn on Adam like a school of sharks in a feeding frenzy.

"They'll start delving around into Adam's past right along with yours. And that means dredging up the fire that killed his wife. It's still considered an open case, Kelly. Do you really want to put him through that again?"

Kelly's mind was racing. Publicly exposing her own involvement in the accident that claimed the life of her father was one thing. Kelly had lived with scandal before, she could survive it again if she had to. But ripping open Adam's wounds about his wife's tragic death was something else.

"I see you're starting to get the picture." Whitney's green eyes narrowed. "The emotional damage this would cause Adam will be devastating enough. But that's not all.

"If even a hint of a scandal develops, you know Adam will feel responsible. After all, Adam was the one who hired you—against the recommendation of his superiors. If they find out that you have these kinds of skeletons in your closet, they'll demand both your resignations."

Kelly recognized the truth in what Whitney was saying. Bad publicity was one of the reasons she'd been forced to leave the *Detroit Gazette*. It was also the reason she'd just volunteered to resign from the *Journal*.

"No newsman with an ounce of integrity will jeopardize the credibility of his paper. . .which means Adam will feel compelled to resign. And even if he doesn't offer to leave, you can bet the corporation that owns the *Journal* won't think twice about firing him. Adam almost lost his job last year when all the publicity about the death of his wife hit the papers."

"You're bluffing!" Kelly retorted.

"If you don't believe me, just ask Jason. The C.E.O. approached him about taking over temporarily when they asked Adam to take a leave of absence last year. If they were that concerned about him then, how do you think this bit of news will hit them?"

Kelly hadn't even considered that. She had had little contact with the corporate executives since she signed on with the *Journal*. She'd met a vice-president once, but since the corporation owned nine newspapers in three states, top management stayed pretty much out of the day-to-day affairs of the individual organizations.

"Think it over, Kelly." Whitney rose and stretched with feline femininity. "I'm sure, if you really *do* care about Adam, you'll do the right thing. It shouldn't be too hard to break it off now. But the longer you wait, the greater the chance of someone leaking the information. I hope you get my drift."

Kelly got her drift all right. "What's in it for you, Whitney?" she asked.

"Adam. With you out of his life, he'll be mine again."

"You're crazy if you really believe that," Kelly said. "He never was 'yours' and he'll never turn to you, even if I am out of the picture. He doesn't love you, Whitney."

"He'll learn to love me once we're together. You see, Jordan, I love him. More important, I know what he's been through and I know what he needs. *I* was the one who was there for him when his wife died. Not you. *I* was the one who helped him pick up the pieces. And he'd be with me right now, if you hadn't come along and turned him against me.

"You have one week to break it off," Whitney added. "The choice is yours. But I warn you, I'll do anything I have to do to get Adam back."

Whitney turned and was gone.

. . .She's like a fighting bull. Adam's words returned to haunt Kelly. *Whitney will be looking for a way to get even with you. She'll go charging off after you and she won't care who she*

126

hurts in the process.

If it was only *her* past, *her* reputation, Kelly wouldn't have given another thought to Whitney's demands. But if Adam was right—if Whitney would destroy anyone, even the man she claimed to love, just to get back at her—Kelly wouldn't be able to live with herself.

Kelly spent the next few hours in turmoil. In one instant, she was white hot with anger. Whitney's veiled threats choked at her heart. How dare Whitney try to blackmail her!

In the next instant, a picture of Adam's anguished face would rise in her mind and scenes of top corporation executives demanding Adam's resignation would follow.

How can I ask Adam to go through another cross-examination of that fatal fire? she asked herself a thousand times. *How can I allow this town to exhume the remains of all our foolish mistakes...dissect and examine our pain?*

The questions tumbled around in her head.

No, Kelly finally decided. She couldn't let herself be responsible for causing him any more pain.

Once the decision was made, Kelly knew she had to do it immediately or she would surely lose her nerve.

Kelly washed her face in cold water, then got ready for work. She arrived at the newspaper before the rest of the crew. But Adam was already in his office. Kelly knocked on the glass door and entered. With trembling lips, told him she thought they'd made an error in judgment in mixing their professional and personal lives.

"It just can't work," she said, her voice dry and colorless. "Now that I've had time to step back and analyze what happened last night, I realize that there are—other considerations."

"And just what *do* you think happened last night?" Confusion flecked Adam's metallic eyes. "I thought we shared something personal and positive and wonderful. What other considerations could there be?"

"Yes. What we shared was all those things. But that doesn't

mean it's right for us to make more out of it than there is."

"What are you trying to say, Kelly? That you felt nothing for me last night? That you feel nothing for me right now?"

"No. I–I'm simply saying that I–I think it's wrong for us to get too emotionally involved with each other right now."

"I already *am* involved, Kelly," Adam responded, a little harshly. "And from your actions last night, I got the distinct impression you wanted to be involved with me, too."

She turned away from him. "Then I was wrong, okay?"

"No, it's not okay!" Adam grabbed her by the elbows and swung her around.

Kelly reeled against the impact of emotions that exploded at his touch. She fought to extinguish the flame before she succumbed to it.

"Adam, please! I–I'm just—scared."

"Scared? Of what?" Adam asked, his voice softening.

"I–I don't know. . . . Maybe I'm afraid things will turn out like they did between Vince and me."

"That could only happen if you didn't feel anything more for me than you did for Vince. Is that what you're trying to say, Kelly? That you think of me the same way you think of Vince Rosselli? Just another lost soul you need to rescue? Well, I don't buy it!"

He pulled her close. "Tell me you don't feel the love between us. Look in my eyes and tell me you feel nothing but benign Christian concern for me!"

An electric charge swept through every nerve ending in Kelly's body. She tried desperately to release him from her mind. . .from her emotions, but her heart wouldn't do what her head told her.

She couldn't meet his gaze; she was afraid Adam would see the agony in her eyes. And she was afraid to look in his without losing the resolve she had managed to muster up.

"Kelly, please. . .tell me the truth. What's happened since we talked last night?"

Hearing the tenderness and the compassion in his voice, Kelly's resolve disintegrated.

"I can't lie to you," she began. "But I can't go on like this, either, or else Whitney will. . . ." She stopped short, uncertain whether or not to go on.

Adam decided for her. "Or else Whitney will do what?" His hold tightened on her arms.

"Or else Whitney will go public with both our pasts," she finished, tears welling in her eyes. "I can't let that happen," she added. "I can't make you live through all the pain of losing your wife again."

"Don't you think you should let me decide for myself how much pain I can take?" he asked gently. "I can handle Whitney, and I can handle the pain, Kelly. I don't need your protection."

"Just like I didn't need your protection from Vince?" Kelly's mouth twisted in a wry smile.

"It's not the same thing, and you know it," Adam admonished lightly.

"Maybe not, but there was some truth in one thing Whitney said. The corporation will not look kindly upon our situation. . . ."

"Then maybe it's time we left the corporation."

His statement sent Kelly's eyes wide with astonishment.

"Did I surprise you? Yes, I guess so. Well, the truth is, I've even surprised myself. I've been doing a lot of thinking lately. I've been re-evaluating my life and the direction I've been going, and I've discovered I've been going nowhere. And I've been thinking that maybe it's time I did some changing."

Just as Kelly started to press for details, Adam's intercom buzzed. It was Maggie. Jason was on line two. Adam put him on conference call so Kelly could hear what he had to say.

"Adam, is Kelly available?" Jason's voice carried over the fuzz of his cellular phone.

"Yes," Kelly responded before Adam could answer. "I'm right here with Adam."

"I need you right now," Jason replied. "I'm at the scene of another fire. This time it looks like they may have caught our arsonist red-handed. They just took her into custody."

"Her?" Adam questioned.

"Yes," Jason answered. "They took Whitney Hewitt in a few minutes ago for questioning. Seems she tried to start the storage compartment in the basement of Kelly's apartment building on fire and got caught in the attempt by the flames. It's okay, Kelly. She didn't get very far. Apparently Dr. Manning discovered the blaze almost immediately and took steps to put it out."

It took a moment for Jason's words to register in Kelly's brain and even then, the full impact didn't hit until she was in her car and on her way home.

15

Kelly felt weird taking pictures of her own apartment building. There hadn't been a whole lot of damage, but Kelly wanted to get a shot of the basement area where Whitney had been trapped and also a couple of Dr. Manning, who had been credited with rescuing Whitney as well as solving the arson fire mystery.

It didn't take her long to accomplish her goal, and Kelly was glad it was over with quickly because her next stop was the police station. Jason was just emerging from the gray stone building when Kelly arrived.

"She ain't confessin'," Jason informed her. "She swears she's not the arsonist. Whitney says she smelled smoke coming from the lower level of the apartment and was shoved into the basement when she went to investigate. I don't believe her though. Ever since she hooked up with Rosselli over at the *Chronicle* I've been suspicious of her."

"Why?"

"Because of the inside track they seem to have on the arson investigation. They seem to know more than even McClanahan would be able to tell them.

"Besides, everyone knows she blames you for her dismissal.

And Whitney, herself, admitted she was at your apartment today for the express purpose of gathering evidence against you. She claims she received an anonymous tip that concerned your involvement in some accident. . . ."

Jason paused purposefully, hoping Kelly would respond. But Kelly deliberately let the statement slide. She had the feeling the whole story would come out soon enough the way it was.

"Only thing is," Jason continued, "the police don't have any physical evidence to connect her with the other fires.

"Say, Kelly, you never did tell me the whole story of what happened at the old apartment building last night. You didn't happen to come across anything useful to the investigation, did you?"

Kelly shook her head. "I didn't find anything except some sort of ring. I never did get a chance to see what it was, though. Vincent interrupted me and then McClanahan barred me from the premises so I couldn't go back."

"And you never found the missing film from the Freeman Factory either?"

"Nope."

"That's too bad. It might have helped convict Whitney."

"There's still no motive, though, Jason."

"Well, maybe she did it for the publicity. Or maybe she did it purely for revenge."

"That's a long way to go just to get back at me, Jason," Kelly discounted the theory.

"I'm not just talking about you," Jason answered. "Some people are even drawing a connection between Whitney and the fire that killed Helen Wentworth."

Kelly gasped. "Why?!"

"Whitney was just as jealous of her as she is of you. . .both professionally and personally. There's been speculation that Whitney started with Helen and just went crazy—became a real pyromaniac. No, sir, I wouldn't put anything past her.

"You know, it could have been Whitney who stole your film of the Freeman Factory fire, too. After all, she and Rosselli were snooping around your desk that same evening you were drugged. That's why I kicked them out. Maybe she thought there was something incriminating on it."

Jason's theory made sense. At least most of it did. But there still weren't any hard facts to go on. The police realized the same thing and within 24 hours, Whitney Hewitt was released due to insufficient evidence. It didn't take her long to let everyone know she was free, either.

Whitney had no sooner been released than the rumors began to fly about Kelly's past. And it only took a day after that for the Executive Vice-President of the corporation to call Adam and demand a complete accounting of the situation.

Adam told the VP the facts as he knew them and offered his own resignation if the company so desired. After hearing Adam out, the vice-president said he'd take it 'under consideration,' then hung up.

Kelly wasn't quite so calm with Jason's questions, however, when he interviewed her for the *Journal*'s story. The interview started out shakily, but Kelly was encouraged by Jason's businesslike attitude.

He stuck to facts, was brief with his questions, and never probed too personally into her emotional state of mind at the time of the accident. All in all, she felt the story he did on her was extremely fair and quite reserved—by Jason's standards.

She thanked him afterward for being so kind and gentle with her, and he actually blushed. It was a side of Jason she hadn't seen before—or had even expected to see. She only hoped this new Jason would continue to grow and mature.

Ever since Kelly had been assigned to work with him on this case, she'd felt the friendship growing between them, even though there was still an aloofness about him that didn't let her get too close. He never discussed his relationship with Maggie, even after Kelly told him she knew they were both in the same foster home at one time. And when she mentioned his illness, he'd gotten downright hostile.

Still, he smiled more now, even laughed out loud once or twice, and seemed more at ease with her than at any time since she'd first come to Bingham. Maybe that was what finally gave her the courage to ask him to come to the Bible study with her and Kevin and Maggie. Jason balked at the idea at first, but after a little prodding from Maggie, he finally consented.

Jason insisted on driving and arrived promptly at 7:30 to pick Kelly up the evening of the study. She met him on the first floor landing. He helped Kelly on with her coat and turned to hold the door for her when they were stopped short by a commotion erupting from the top of the stairs.

The thump, crash and loud moan sent them both racing up the steps to be greeted by the sight of Dr. Manning embedded in the potted palm used to adorn the hallway of the second floor landing.

Kelly had to stifle the chortle that forced its way into her throat at the sight. Dear Dr. Manning, one foot in the planter, one on the top of the stair, glasses askew and hair entangled in the palm fronds, sat spitting and sputtering as he struggled to extricate himself from his predicament.

"Who moved the potted plant!" he bellowed.

"I guess the janitor finally got around to cleaning up after the fire," Kelly offered.

"It would've been nice if he would have replaced the lightbulbs in the hallways at the same time so we could see around this obstacle course he created!" the doctor said indignantly.

Kelly couldn't restrain herself. "Here," she giggled as she offered him her hand. "Let us help you out of there before you take root."

She and Jason each took a hand and tugged heavily, lifting the older gentleman to his feet. He seemed to be all arms and legs, but finally they had him back upright.

"You didn't hurt anything, did you?" Kelly inquired.

"Nothing but my pride."

"Are you sure?" Kelly helped him brush the dirt off his jacket.

"Miss Jordan, I *am* a doctor. I should know if I'm hurt," he said, pulling as much dignity as he could muster around himself. "Really. I'm all right. I assure you."

"You did take quite a spill, sir," Jason pointed out. "We don't want to take any chances when it comes to your health."

Dr. Manning squinted up at Jason, recognizing him for the first time. "Seems to me, young man, I've told you the same thing on a number of occasions."

Jason paled. "My health is not the issue here, Dr. Manning. Yours is." The words were clipped off in a stiff, rigid staccato. "We were just trying to make sure you didn't break any bones or sprain an ankle or something."

"Thanks for your concern, but as you can see. . ." he wriggled his hands and feet, "I've still got all my parts and they're all still working. And I can see I've interrupted your evening. So please, go on now. I'll be fine!"

"Well, we were just on our way out," Kelly admitted. "But if you need a lift or anything, we'll be happy to oblige."

"No. No. I was just on my way to the Sunshine Home. This is my volunteer night. I need to change coats, then I'll be on my way. So, you kids scoot!" He shooed them down the steps.

As the couple stepped out into the night, Kelly turned to her escort with a quizzical look. "I didn't know you were acquainted with Dr. Manning."

"I know him."

Jason's reply did not invite further discussion, but Kelly pressed on anyway.

"Have you known him long?"

"Long enough." Jason guided her toward his car. "Did you hear he's been nominated for Bingham's Man-of-the-Year Award?

"I've arranged to get an exclusive with him for the paper.

135

They'll announce the winner the day before the Awards Banquet so the recipient has a chance to prepare a presentation. I was hoping I could get you to do the photos for this assignment."

Jason's diversionary tactics were so slick, Kelly didn't realize she'd been sidestepped until minutes later. And Jason made sure she never got a chance to return to the topic the rest of the evening.

The study went smoothly. Adam was working late, so Kelly sat with Jason, but he didn't say very much. However, Kelly hadn't expected him to.

Maggie, Kevin, Jason, and Kelly stopped for coffee afterward, and Jason was on his best behavior. He tried to keep the atmosphere light and entertaining, and Kelly found herself relaxing and opening up to him a little by the time they'd finished their second cup of coffee.

Maybe Jason really is changing, she thought to herself. The last few times she'd been in his company had been decidedly pleasant.

He'd proved himself a gentleman and a friend on several occasions and, although she knew he was not a Christian, agreeing to attend the Bible study was a good sign he might at least be open to the possibility of hearing the gospel.

She found herself daydreaming a bit. . .envisioning the day that Jason might come to know the Lord.

"So what do you think?"

Kelly jerked up. She could feel a crimson curtain rising in her cheeks. "I'm sorry. I wasn't listening. What did you say?"

"I said, who do you think's going to be Reporter-of-the-Year?" repeated Jason.

"Well, you, of course," she laughed nervously.

"Good answer," Jason replied, a pleased smile on his face.

They finished their coffee, then Jason drove Kelly home. He saw her to her door, but didn't ask to come in, although she thought he might have done so if Dr. Manning hadn't returned just then. At the sight of him, Jason quickly turned to leave.

Kelly called out goodnight to him, but he made no reply. She did, however, hear him ask the doctor if he was okay.

"Yes. I'm fine," he reassured Jason.

"Well, you take care of yourself," Jason admonished.

"I will, if you promise to do the same. . . ."

Jason started down the steps.

"And don't forget to take your medication as ordered," Dr. Manning called out after him.

"Curious," Kelly murmured as she turned the key in the lock. "Very curious, indeed."

16

The holiday rush reached its peak that week, and the *Journal* was very shorthanded. Adam hadn't found a replacement for Whitney, so Kelly ended up working through most of the holidays.

If that wasn't enough, there was always Whitney to worry about. The *Tri-County Chronicle* spewed out article after article on Kelly and Adam. They even did an informal probe into the fire that killed Helen Wentworth. But it was short-lived since nothing new was uncovered. But in the midst of the furor, Adam and Kelly decided not to date until it all died down.

Fortunately, no one demanded Adam's resignation over the *Chronicle* articles, although Jason hinted he'd be only too happy to take over for Adam if he chose to resign. Kelly knew that the corporation higher-ups might just take him up on it, too, since his series of reports on the arson fires had been receiving a lot of attention from his peers and the public alike.

Jason was a shoo-in for the coveted Reporter-of-the-Year award. Unfortunately, the news seemed to be going to his head, and Jason made it clear to everyone that he felt he warranted special attention. He didn't go back to the Bible study.

It didn't help, either, that Jason frequently provoked the

managing editor by ignoring Adam's orders. The skirmishes were often brief and usually ended with Adam pulling rank. But once or twice Kelly found herself caught in the middle of their disputes, both men urging her to take their side of the issue.

Jason also seemed to be missing more and more work due to illness which didn't do much to improve his standing with Adam. But when Jason was there, his cockiness made him difficult to work with. Time and again, Kelly heard Jason grumble about "the abuse an award-winning reporter has to take from rank amateurs."

The morning of the Tri-County News Awards banquet, the offices of the *Journal* crackled with excitement. Even Kelly had to admit she was getting caught up in the drama and suspense. It was the first time she'd ever been up for an award, and she was a little surprised to discover how much she cared about the possibility of winning.

The company gossip had Adam pegged as Editor-of-the-Year and predicted that Jason would receive the Action Series Award among others. Dr. Manning had, indeed, been named Man-of-the-Year. Kelly hadn't known, however, until Jason's interview with him, just how richly he deserved that distinction. In the background information Jason had dug up for the interview, he had discovered that the doctor was a rather remarkable man and an extremely generous philanthropist.

The Sunshine Home, a group foster care facility designed for underprivileged children and kids with special needs, had been a primary recipient of his generosity, although several scholarships and medical endowments had been made in his name as well. But money wasn't the only contribution Dr. Manning had made.

The physician was known to spend his free afternoons and two nights a week caring for the poor, the homeless, and the destitute at the local free clinic.

The doctor appeared visibly embarrassed, even baffled, by all the attention he was generating.

"I'm a simple man with simple needs," he maintained during the interview with Jason. "I'm not married, don't have a large family. What do I need a lot of money for? Isn't it better that the money be out there doing someone some good?"

Most of the interview followed the same course of questions and responses. As Jason and Kelly were wrapping up the session, Adam came over to offer his congratulations.

"I'm looking forward to your speech tonight," Adam commented as he shook the older gentleman's hand.

"Well, I'm not!" Dr. Manning grimaced. "And maybe after you hear it, you'll wish they hadn't asked me to speak at all."

"Dr. Manning, I'm sure you'll do just fine," Kelly said as she snapped a few last photos of the doctor, then walked over to her desk to reload her camera. "Besides, we'll all be there to lend you moral support."

Kelly fished around in one of her desk drawers, pulling out a fresh roll of film.

"Good grief!" The doctor smacked his forehead with the heel of his hand. "I almost forgot again! Here." He pulled something out of his pocket and handed it to Kelly. "I found that the night I tangled with the palm tree. Been meaning to return it to you ever since, but kept forgetting. It's a film canister, I think. Figured it had to be yours."

Kelly turned the plastic container over in her hand and pulled off the cap. She knew before ever reading the label that it had to be the missing film of the Freeman Factory fire.

"I've been looking weeks for this!" Kelly exclaimed. "I've searched everywhere! Combed my entire apartment. Even looked around the door and along the steps. It must have fallen in the potted palm!"

"That's what I thought. With it being so dark in there, no one would ever have noticed it, if I hadn't fallen over that confounded plant."

"Oh, Dr. Manning, I can't tell you how grateful I am that you found this. The pictures on this film could be the key to solving a very big puzzle. It may even contain the evidence we need to convict—or absolve—Whitney Hewitt of arson. I'm going to go develop this roll right now."

Kelly headed for the darkroom, but as she opened the door, Maggie let out a bloodcurdling scream. Kelly swung around just in time to see Jason turn as white as the proverbial sheet and hit the floor.

17

Maggie was already down at his side by the time Kelly reached them.

"Maggie! What happened?"

"I–I don't know." She looked up at Kelly, tears brimming her eyes. "He was just standing there, when all of a sudden his eyes glazed and rolled up and then, bam, he just dropped over."

"It looks like a seizure." Dr. Manning was kneeling beside them. He took off his coat, rolling it into a makeshift pillow for Jason and slipped it under his head. "Somebody call an ambulance and get me my bag. It's out in the car."

Adam reached for the phone and Kevin took off for the door.

The doctor had just begun his examination when a tremor swept through Jason's body. He convulsed twice more, then lay still.

"Is he going to be all right?" Maggie was crying.

"Don't you worry, little lady." Dr. Manning patted Maggie's hand. "These epileptic seizures always look worse than they really are. They're more scary than anything else. The main thing is to make sure he didn't hurt himself when he went down."

"Are you saying that Jason is an epileptic?" Adam asked the

142

question that was on everyone's mind.

Dr. Manning looked up, surprised. "You mean Jason never told you? Well, I guess I should have figured he wouldn't. He's always been one of my more difficult patients. Never paying attention to anything I tell him. I have to struggle with him just to get him to take his medication. I wouldn't be a bit surprised to learn he had forgotten to take it today and that's what brought on this seizure."

Kevin had returned with the doctor's medical bag and the physician immediately began his examination.

"Maggie, did you know about this?" Kelly drew her friend aside.

There was no response and that, along with the guilty look in Maggie's downcast eyes, confirmed her complicity in Jason's secret.

"You mean you knew about this all along and you didn't tell anyone?! Didn't you realize how dangerous this could be?"

"He–he made me promise not to tell," Maggie sobbed. "Jason's had seizures almost all his life, but until the last couple of months, the medication's always kept them under control. I–I didn't think it was necessary for you all to know. It wasn't up to me to say anything."

"And what do you think would have happened if he'd been covering a story when he got one of them? He could have been seriously injured, maybe even killed." Adam took up the tirade.

"If I had known about Jason's physical problems, I would have been a little more selective in the assignments I handed over to him."

"But don't you see," Maggie's voice quavered, "that's exactly why he didn't want you or anyone else to know. He was afraid you would all think he wasn't able to do his job. Or worse, that you would pity him."

"I'm not going to lie to you, Maggie. Knowing about Jason's illness would have made a difference in how I dealt with him, but I would like to believe I would have treated him like I would

143

treat any professional. More importantly, if I had known from the beginning about all of this, maybe I could have helped. Maybe we could have avoided this whole situation."

Maggie was crying in earnest now, afraid not only for Jason but for herself as well. "I'm sorry. Please don't be angry with me, and please don't be angry with Jason, either. He only wanted to do his job without people babying him or making fun of him."

Adam's voice softened. "I understand that, Maggie, and I promise you neither of your jobs is in jeopardy because of this incident. But you have to remember that as Managing Editor of this newspaper, I'm responsible for all of you." Adam's pale eyes left Maggie for a moment and fixed on Kelly.

Jason moved and groaned just then and Maggie went back to him. Kelly stood beside Adam and watched as Dr. Manning struggled to bring Jason around.

"It's not your fault, Adam. You didn't know," Kelly said soothingly.

"I should have guessed." There was a weariness in Adam's voice. "He's been sick so often lately, and he always seemed so agitated whenever I asked him what was wrong. I should have been more caring, more concerned. Maybe then I would have figured out that there was something physically wrong with him."

"You're not a doctor, Adam. How could you have possibly known Jason had epilepsy?"

"I appreciate what you're trying to do. But the fact of the matter is, I didn't want to know the truth. I have a confession to make, Kelly. The last couple of weeks, I've noticed how close the two of you have become. I was jealous, and I let those feelings color my attitude toward him. As a result, I missed every signal he sent out because of it. Instead of asking why he was acting the way he was, I just got angry."

Kelly painfully met his gaze, knowing she shared his guilt. Maybe even more so since she'd known all along there was something wrong. Her heart was heavy as she broke away from Adam's eyes and went to put an arm around Maggie.

By the time the ambulance arrived, Jason was already coming around.

Dr. Manning insisted on taking him to the hospital for more tests, but said as he left that he didn't expect to find anything seriously wrong, especially after confirming that Jason had, indeed, neglected to take his medication that morning.

After Jason was safely on his way to the hospital, Kelly turned gloomily back to the darkroom to complete the task she had started before all the excitement began.

A few moments ago, she had been riding a tide of exhilaration. The prospect of discovering the true identity of their arsonist had sent the adrenalin flowing, but now—now her heart was no longer in her detective work.

Kelly entered the darkroom, closing the door behind her. She snapped off the overhead light and switched on the red work light. The crimson bulb bathed the room in blood-orange shadows. Usually the odd coloring didn't bother her, but today its effects added to her uneasiness. She gave the roll of film its first chemical bath then stepped back to inspect her work.

She sensed more than heard a presence in the room. Kelly froze. The unidentified body moved toward her.

"It's just me, Kelly," Adam announced.

Kelly let out an audible sigh of relief.

"I hope I didn't startle you. I was checking on some other photos when you came in, and I didn't want to ruin your pictures by going out the door."

"I guess Jason's seizure really got to me." Kelly grinned sheepishly. "For a minute there, I had the horrible notion that the arsonist had found out about these pictures and had come to rub them—and me—out."

"Well, thanks a lot," Adam teased her as he turned his attention to the examination of the color shots. Suddenly, his brow furrowed and his jaw set.

145

"What's this?" He pointed at one shot in particular with the tip of his pen.

Kelly peered at the picture of the rising sunburst over the roof of the Freeman Factory. Down in the corner appeared a fuzzy shadow, clearly a human figure, but distant and dark.

"I don't know," she said. "It looks like a person. See? Here—you can almost see a face." She squinted again trying to distinguish the features.

"Can you blow this up? Enhance it?"

"I can, but it'll take some time."

"Make it your number one priority."

18

Kelly didn't leave the darkroom or newsroom until she took a break with Maggie at noon to visit Jason at the hospital. An orderly had just brought him back from the lab where they had conducted a few routine tests. Everything had checked out okay, and Maggie was visibly relieved when she heard the news.

However, Jason's face was pale and drawn when they entered his room. He seemed exceptionally nervous at first sight of them, almost as if he expected them to attack, especially when Maggie ran to him and flung her arms around his neck.

"It's okay!" Maggie blurted out. "Everyone knows and no one's angry with you. Not even Adam."

Kelly read the alarm in Jason's eyes and started to speak, but Maggie rattled on.

"He really isn't upset about the epilepsy. Honest. Although he wasn't too happy about us keeping it a secret from him. But I really don't think he's going to stop you from going out on assignments. He promised he wouldn't make a big deal out of it, and I think he meant it."

Kelly saw Jason heave a sigh of relief. He smiled weakly at Maggie and patted her hand. "Thanks," he said simply to her, then directed his next words to Kelly.

"Guess I must have given you all quite a scare. Sorry about that. I hope you can forgive me for not telling you about the seizures, Kelly. The truth is, I was just plain embarrassed to let anyone know."

"I know it hasn't been easy for you, Jason," Kelly reassured him. "I just wish you could have trusted me with the truth. I really do think I would have understood."

Jason avoided Kelly's eyes and changed the subject. "So, are you all going to the party tonight? Wish I could be there."

"Well, to tell the truth, I'm not so sure I want to go after everything that's happened," Kelly remarked.

"Oh, no!" Maggie protested. "You just have to come, Kel. I'm depending on you to help me get ready. I can't do a thing with my hair, and I don't have the slightest idea what to wear to something like this. Please? Please say you'll come."

Kelly could hardly refuse. "Okay. . .okay. But if I am going tonight, we better get back to work right now. I'm having all kinds of problems developing that film, and I want that done before I leave."

Jason's eyes lit up at the reference to the film. "Sounds like you've found something," he probed. "You think we'll finally be able to put Whitney behind bars where she belongs?"

"I don't know for sure," she answered. "I may have something on one shot, but we're going to need to blow it up at least twice and enhance it before I can tell for sure. At any rate, it's going to take awhile, so, come on, Mags, let's get going." She tugged at Maggie's sleeve and headed for the door.

"Well, good luck," Jason called after them.

"Time to go, Kel," Maggie called from outside the darkroom door. "It's almost five o'clock."

"Already? I can't leave now. I just have one more enhancement to do, and I should have a pretty good idea of who's crouching in the corner on this picture."

19

Kelly snatched her hand away with such force she nearly whacked a man standing behind her. She felt a stab of fear and anger and a dozen other emotions shoot through her heart, but quickly forced the feelings aside with cold, crisp determination.

She would take her vow seriously. This man was forgiven. No matter what he had done to her, he *was* forgiven. It might take her awhile to get used to that idea, and, she knew now that feelings of forgiveness wouldn't automatically come. Like the clapper of a bell, she couldn't expect the ringing to stop immediately after releasing the rope, but she could anticipate the clanging to grow dimmer and dimmer with time.

She gathered herself together.

"Vincent," she managed to say with civility. "I'm glad you're here tonight. I have something to say to you."

"Oh, really? I thought we said all we had to say the last time we met," he sneered. "You made yourself quite clear, then, how you feel about me." His eyes burned with hatred.

Kelly noticed Adam move in beside her as Whitney appeared alongside Vincent. The showdown had come. Kelly swallowed hard.

"I want to apologize to you," she said. "My behavior toward you ever since my father died has been cruel and vengeful, and I've no right to act that way. I accept full responsibility for all the pain I've caused you. I know that's not much of a consolation, but I *am* sorry. Would–would you forgive me?"

For the first time since she'd met him, Vincent was speechless. His expression was one of complete bewilderment.

Whitney, however, was not impressed.

"If you think your little contrived apology is going to stop us from evening up the score, Kelly, you're sadly mistaken."

Whitney's jade eyes sparked with revenge. The picture she portrayed in her shimmering sequined gown of rich emerald green was one of power and fury and wild animal rage.

"I wouldn't issue any threats, if I were you, Whitney," Adam interrupted. "After everything you and your accomplice have pulled in the last few months, you'd be very foolish to do any more damage to other people."

"We haven't 'pulled' anything." Whitney tossed her windswept hair in defiance. "We've simply exposed the truth about both of you. And we'll go on exposing the truth."

"And what's that supposed to mean?" Adam demanded.

"That means this town hasn't heard anything yet!" Rosselli interjected, finding his voice. "But they will. By tomorrow, every household that gets the *Chronicle* will know that you two are the top two suspects in the arson case!"

His words hit Kelly like a pail of ice water. She hadn't thought it possible for Vincent Rosselli to cause any more mischief, but leave it to the master to come up with something like this.

Adam just laughed. "You've got to be out of your cotton-picking mind. You'll never get anyone to believe that."

"Don't be so sure, Wentworth. I've kept this a secret so far because I've had no choice. But George McClanahan knows Whitney isn't the arsonist. She had no motive, no opportunity, and no connections with this string of fires. Now Kelly and you–especially you–on the other hand, have been involved in this whole thing right from the start. The timing. . .your motives. . .you two always showing up at the scenes of the crimes. . . .

"McClanahan has suspected you two right from the start, but he insisted it would impede his investigation if I let on that you two were under suspicion. Up until now, I've needed him as a source for my articles, so I've bided my time. But I've waited long enough. I don't need McClanahan any more. You two have provided me with enough ammunition to put you away for good.

"Between your snooping around the fires and the missing evidence, plus the fact that Kelly arrived in town just before the arson fires started up, I don't think I'll have much trouble getting people to see the picture," he said triumphantly.

"What an interesting choice of words, Rosselli," Adam returned. "You're absolutely right. Come tomorrow, a lot of people might be 'seeing the picture.' The picture Kelly took, that is."

"What are you talking about?" Whitney's eyes narrowed.

"We found the film."

"What film?" Rosselli demanded.

"The missing film, Vincent. The film of the Freeman Factory fire site."

"But that film was destroyed!"

"The roll of black and white film was. But Kelly had a whole color roll that was missing—until yesterday, that is."

"You're lying." Vince drew out the words, inviting further information.

"What's the matter, Vince?" Adam obliged. "Thought you had all the bases covered? You seem kind of nervous. Is there something on that film you don't want anyone to see? Evidence perhaps...or possibly the arsonist himself? You know, Kelly has just one more enhancement to run that film through, but when she's done, we should have a pretty clear idea of who's been setting fires the last couple of months.

"Interesting, isn't it? You've been here just as long as Kelly. You've somehow managed to win George McClanahan's trust and turn him off to all the rest of us journalists at the same time. And now, lo and behold, you're up for a Tri-County News Award for *your* coverage of the arsonist. What an amazing series of coincidences!"

"Now hold on just one minute!" Rosselli exploded. "I've got nothing to do with those fires. And if you go around making those kinds of allegations, you'd better have the proof to back them up!"

"Unlike you," Adam shot back, "I *never* make public accusations without evidence." Adam grabbed Kelly's arm and escorted her to their table. Kevin and Maggie were waiting for them there, along with several other staff members of the *Journal*.

Kelly felt drained after their exchange with Vince and Whitney, and she was more than a little anxious at the thought of how they would react to Adam's accusations. She couldn't concentrate at all on dinner even though the meal was delicious: top tenderloin steak, twice-baked potatoes, fresh broccoli, and chocolate mousse.

Her mind kept drifting back to Adam's conclusions. Could he be right? Was Vince involved in the arson case? Would he have gone so far as to deliberately start fires, just to get an exclusive story?

Then again, it may not have been just the story Vince was after, Kelly reasoned. Vince had been hoping the prestige of an award-winning story could still get him the job as publisher of the *Chronicle*.

And if it *was* true, had they made a big mistake in tipping him off about the pictures? An uneasy feeling roller coastered under Kelly's ribs and stayed with her during Dr. Manning's Man-of-the-Year acceptance speech. When they took a break before the awards presentations, Kelly excused herself. She

156

had to call the office. She had to be sure those photographs were safe.

Kelly let the phone ring more than a dozen times before she finally hung up. She knew the printing of tomorrow's issue should have been completed, but there was usually someone there to keep an eye on things even after the presses had been shut down for the night.

It could be that whoever was on duty was out of earshot or tied up with something he couldn't leave. It didn't necessarily mean anything was wrong. Still. . .

Kelly started back to her table, got half-way there, then decided to try once more to reach someone by phone. She made her way back to the lobby. As she turned the corner, she heard a familiar voice. Vincent was on the phone she'd just left.

"I'm telling you, McClanahan, she's got pictures. . . ."

Kelly gasped, then dove back around the corner.

"Now why would they lie about something like that?" Vince paused. "Well, I don't care. If it is true, they're going to blow everything. I suggest you get off your big duff and check their story out!" Vince slammed down the receiver and Kelly took off for her table.

She found Kevin just before she reached her table and asked to borrow his car keys.

"I left something very important at the office," she said in way of explanation. "I've got to have it right away, but I promise, I'll be right back."

Kevin looked baffled, but handed her his keys.

"You sure you don't want me to go along?"

"No, really. There's no need for both of us to go. Besides, someone's got to pick up all those awards we're going to win tonight, right?" She laughed, but she knew it sounded high and nervous. Turning quickly, she left the country club grounds in just minutes.

When Kevin returned to the table, Adam asked him where

Kelly was going. "I saw her heading for the stairs. Is anything wrong?"

"No," Kevin replied. "She said she'd be back in a few minutes. She borrowed my car to go get something."

The master of ceremonies suddenly called out Adam's name and the *Journal* as the winners of the Action Series Award given to Kelly Jordan and Jason Roberts. Startled, he moved to accept the awards, but his mind wasn't on the ceremony any longer. The few minutes dragged into an hour. Finally, Adam had a chance to continue his questioning of Kevin.

"Kevin, Kelly's been gone more than a few minutes. Where did she go?"

"Back to the office. She said she'd left something important there."

Adam felt the color drain from his face. He grabbed Kevin's arm and forced his voice to a calmness he didn't feel.

"Something hasn't felt quite right all evening," Adam said. "Now I'm sure something's wrong. Vince knows about the photos—I bet Kelly's gone back to get them. Let's go. I don't want her there this late at night by herself. Not now."

Kevin agreed. "But let's not alarm Maggie, okay?" he pleaded. "We can tell her something's come up and we have to go back to the office. We can drop her off at her place first."

Adam nodded in agreement, but Maggie wasn't quite so cooperative when they talked with her.

"I don't see why we had to leave so early!" she said as she slid into the front seat of Adam's car. "And where did Kelly go with the Cherry Bomb, Kevin?"

"I told you before. Something came up at the office and Kelly went to check it out," Kevin explained from the back seat. "She hasn't come back as soon as she said she would, so we kind of figured she needed some extra help, and we're going to see if we can give her a hand," he finished.

"Well, why can't I come with you?" Maggie pouted.

"Because it might take quite a while to straighten things out,"

Adam told her. "Now, just sit back and enjoy the ride, okay? And, by the way, can you move Jason's plaque? It's wedged in next to the stick shift."

Maggie complied. "This ought to cheer him up," she said. "He was pretty worried this noon that you would fire him or at least make him work a desk job."

"Well, I haven't ruled that out entirely," Adam responded. "I don't know much about his problem except that most epileptics can lead a pretty normal life. But there are a couple of things that worry me about the possibility of him having another episode like the one today. For instance, what if he's driving and he has one of those seizures? I didn't realize an epileptic could even get a driver's license."

"Oh, sure," Maggie explained. "As long as the person is under a doctor's care and taking medication and as long as the medication is controlling the seizures. He just has to have so many clean months—seizure-free months—before he applies for the license. Then, if he passes the regular tests, the state will issue him one.

"That reminds me, though. I was supposed to pick up Jason's prescription and take it over to his apartment so he'd have it first thing in the morning. Do you think we could stop at that all-night drug store on Front Street on the way home?"

"Can't that wait until morning?" Kevin groaned.

"Well, Dr. Manning thought it was pretty important to get it filled tonight. I have the prescription right here in my purse."

She pulled out the slip and read off the medication. "Phenobarbital. That's what he's taking now. Dr. Manning just switched him onto that this last fall. Jason was a little worried when he did that. It's a barbiturate...stronger than what he'd been taking previously. He said it made him dizzy sometimes. That's probably why he didn't always take it like he was supposed to. It also constricts the pupils—and he was scared somebody would be able to tell he was taking something."

"A barbiturate?" Adam slowed the car, then pulled over. "Let me look at that." He took the prescription from her, switched on the courtesy light and stared at the words written there. A shadow of alarm spread across his face. Something had started to click.

20

When Kelly arrived at the *Journal*, only her Mustang and Jason's car remained in the parking lot. She pulled Kevin's Chevy in alongside her car and got out.

"Strange," she said aloud. "Maybe the night guy got sick and couldn't find anyone to cover for him."

She moved toward the building and tried the door. She was surprised to find it unlocked. Slowly turning the knob, she cautiously swung the door open and stepped into the darkened receiving area. She stood still for a minute, listening for any movement. When she heard nothing, she switched on the overhead light. Everything looked quiet.

Kelly went into the newsroom and straight to the darkroom. She tried the door. Locked. Turning, she headed for Adam's office. His door, though normally closed and locked, was standing ajar. Again, she stopped and listened but heard nothing. Warily, she swung the door open and entered the glass enclosed office. She didn't bother to turn on a light; there was enough coming in from the newsroom. She went straight to Adam's desk and slid the calendar out from his desk blotter. Underneath, in the corner, she found the key to the darkroom. Only she and Adam knew where it was kept.

Since she was here, she might as well check on the photos. *It probably wouldn't hurt to take them back to the party, either,* she thought. She didn't feel at all comfortable about leaving them in the office under the present circumstances. She picked up the key and swung around.

"I'll take that."

Kelly jumped at the sound of his voice.

"Good grief! Jason! What are you doing here?"

Kelly realized how stupid that question sounded the minute she opened her mouth. Jason obviously hadn't wanted anyone to know he was there, let alone what he was doing there.

"I need to get into the darkroom," he said as he reached for the key in her hand.

She pulled away from him. "Why?"

"Just give me the key, Kelly."

"Not until you tell me what's going on here. What are you doing out of the hospital? Where's the night guy?"

"I was feeling a lot better tonight, and I insisted the hospital release me. They had no choice but to comply. You know, I could ask you what you're doing here, too. I thought you were going to the awards banquet tonight."

"I was there, and I will be going back shortly. I just wanted to see how my photos came out. Now, you tell me, why are you here? And where is the night watchman?"

"I. . .uh. . .got to thinking about those pictures you're developing, and I wanted to check something out. When I got here, I sent the night man home."

"What did you want to check out?"

"Just something," he said evasively. "Come on. Let me have the key so I can take a look at those photographs."

"We'll both take a look," she said suspiciously.

At first she was afraid he wouldn't let her pass, but when she made a move toward him, he stepped aside. She inserted the key in the latch, keeping one eye on Jason all the time.

She switched on the red light and went over to a corner of the room where the blow-ups were hanging on a line, drying. Jason moved in behind her and a chill ran up her spine. Kelly slipped the key into her evening bag and turned to examine the color photographs.

They stood together a moment, studying the photos in silence. The blow-ups clearly showed a dark figure in the shadows of the building, but the face was still not distinguishable. Kelly reached up and began unsnapping the pictures from the line.

"What are you doing?" Jason asked.

"I'm taking them with me," Kelly replied.

"Wait." Jason caught her by the wrist with an intensity that took Kelly by surprise. When Jason saw her reaction, he released her.

"I'd like to take a closer look at them," he explained.

"But you can't tell who it is the way they are now," Kelly responded. She cautiously returned to her task of removing them. "You can see them tomorrow after I run the enhancement on them. We should be able to see the figure a lot more clearly."

"I can't wait that long!" Jason blurted out. "I mean. . .I'd really like to run the enhancement tonight. Why don't you go on back to the party, and I'll take care of this." He tried to take the pictures from her hand.

"If you're really that anxious to see the blow-ups, I'll finish them myself right now," she persisted.

Jason wavered, then moved back from her. She turned to the chemicals and liquids and film and, laying her purse beside her on the counter, began the enhancement process. Jason stood mute behind her throughout the procedure, his eyes never leaving her. Kelly could feel them burrowing into the back of her head and shuddered. When she finished, she stepped back and picked up her purse.

"It'll take a few minutes for the images to develop," she told Jason.

He shrugged his shoulders. "I can wait."

The tension that had slithered into the room expanded. Kelly eyed Jason warily. He was getting very anxious. She noticed him wringing his hands, like he always did when he got nervous. Only this time, he didn't have his little gold ring to fidget with.

His dark, shiny eyes kept darting back and forth from the photos to her to the digital timer on the wall. Kelly felt her neck stiffen, her shoulders tighten, as they waited for the results to appear on the film.

The room itself seemed to contract as if it were one large muscle. The air grew thick and suffocating and the eerie blood-red light only added to the illusion of being trapped inside a living, breathing being.

What is he looking for? she wondered. *Why is this so important to him?*

She didn't like the answers she kept coming up with.

As the minutes clicked by, Kelly found herself glancing more and more often at the emerging images on the slick paper. She also noticed Jason edging closer and closer toward her. As the face on the photo finally came into focus, the full six-foot-four frame moved in directly beside her. Together they watched as the person in the picture took on form and features.

A lump caught in Kelly's throat, but Jason's reaction was one of pure and simple indifference. That was the strangest thing of all, Kelly thought, that Jason could be so apathetic about the whole thing...for there, staring back at them from the glossy, glistening page was the slightly fuzzy but unmistakable face of Jason Roberts.

Kelly closed her eyes and let out an almost inaudible moan as the significance of the photo hit her.

"It's not like it seems." Jason grabbed her by the arm. "I was investigating the scene, just like you were."

"Then why wait 'til now to tell me about it? Jason, I might be slow, but I'm not stupid. You weren't down there investigating anything. You were down there trying to get rid of

164

evidence....Jason, you *did* get rid of the evidence, didn't you?"

He didn't have to answer. Shock stiffened Kelly's face as the full implications of her discovery began to take shape.

"And that wasn't the only evidence you had to get rid of, was it? *You're* the one who destroyed the first set of pictures. Whitney had nothing to do with it!"

Kelly's mind raced back to the day after the factory fire. The day Whitney was dismissed. The day she'd been drugged, and the day the roll of color film disappeared. Understanding rose in her face.

"These color shots...you tried to get rid of them, too, didn't you?" she demanded.

Jason must have thought the pictures from the fire were still in her camera and removed the fresh roll of film, thinking it was the spent one. If he had ripped the roll out without checking it, wanting only to expose it to light to destroy whatever was on it, he wouldn't have known the difference.

It all began to make sense now. She had told him just before she got sick that she had more pictures. He had even offered to take care of them for her, probably planning to have some unfortunate accident while developing them, but she had refused his help.

How could she have been so duped by him? She had believed he really felt sorry for her that day, that he really wanted to help her out. And all the time, he just wanted to get his hands on the photos. He had acted so sincere about her loss. Offering to reshoot the scenes for her....Sitting with her when she had been so upset about Vince and Whitney....Getting her coffee.... Coffee! The coffee that had made her so ill! Kelly's eyes went wide in alarm.

Think, Kelly, think! She fought to maintain her calm. *This guy could be dangerous. You can't afford to say the wrong thing...do the wrong thing.*

"Why, Jason? Why?" It's the only thing that would come out of her mouth.

"Don't you see?" he asked, as if it was as plain as the picture in front of her. "I had to. It's the only way they would take me seriously."

"Who? Who wouldn't take you seriously—about what?" Kelly struggled to comprehend Jason's twisted thinking.

"All of them: Adam, Whitney, the Awards committee. After that series I did last year, Adam should have made me his senior reporter, but, instead, he made me share everything with Whitney. Can you believe that? Comparing my work with that green-eyed she-devil's!

"She did everything she could to sabotage my work. She stole all the good assignments, berated me in front of my peers, even destroyed some of my best pieces...all because I dumped her. Surely you understand, Kelly. You've been a target of her persecution. You know what it's like."

"And that's why you let Whitney take the blame for destroying my pictures and for putting the drugs in my coffee?"

"Wasn't that ironic?" Jason laughed. "I can't tell you how funny that was. You know, I hadn't planned to get her fired, but it worked out so well!"

"And the fire at my apartment? You started it? You pushed Whitney into the basement and locked the door?"

"Don't look so horrified, Kelly! She had it coming! She'd found out about the epilepsy while we were dating and used it to blackmail me in order to get the choice assignments. Then, when I told her I wasn't going to put up with it anymore, she tried using her influence to turn the Awards Committee against me.

"She thought she was so clever! But I found out what she was trying to do. I had to do something. Find a story they couldn't ignore. The arson series was a natural. It's the only way I could think of to make them see how good a reporter I am. When they read my series, they had to take notice. I showed them! I showed them all!"

"Jason, listen to me." Kelly tried to stay calm. "You didn't have to burn those buildings to the ground to convince us you're a good reporter...we already know that. Why, Adam has told me himself that he thinks you're very talented. Everyone else does, too."

"Sure, *now* they do. But that's only because I proved it by writing that award winning series. Don't you see?" he asked, seemingly frustrated at her slowness. "Nobody believed in me before I started writing the arson story. And I couldn't have written the series if I hadn't created the opportunity."

"Opportunity?" Kelly was incredulous. "We're talking about a serious crime here. Not some business venture. Whitney could have been hurt, maybe even killed!"

A strange expression came over Jason's face. He looked as though he had travelled to some other place, some other time.

"I did everything in my power to make sure that wouldn't happen," he said oddly.

"But what if something would've happened, Jason? If someone would have died in one of those fires, you would have been responsible. It would have been your fault! You'd have been a murderer."

"No!" Jason shouted. "It wasn't my fault! I never wanted Helen to die!"

Kelly's head snapped up at the mention of Helen's name.

"Helen? What does Helen have to do with these latest fires?" Jason's face froze. "Nothing."

"You're not talking about the last three months, are you...?" Kelly searched his face in horror.

Jason was silent.

"You're talking about another fire, aren't you? You're talking about the fire that killed Helen Wentworth."

"It was Adam's own fault!" he said defiantly. "If he had only trusted me that night, everything would have worked out perfectly."

"You mean you set the fire that killed Adam's wife?" Kelly asked, but Jason wasn't listening.

"I could have handled the hostage story. I'm a good reporter," he continued, oblivious to her question. "They should never have stuck me with writing obits. I was ready to take on something bigger! But they wouldn't listen to reason."

"An innocent woman died in that fire, Jason! And her unborn child!"

"She wasn't supposed to be there!"

Jason thrust both hands through his thick brown hair, pulling his fingers through the waves and locking them together at the back of his neck. He stood there a second, scrutinizing her, analyzing her as if she were a creature from another planet. Then he dropped his hands to his sides, opening them up in a pleading gesture.

"How was I supposed to know she'd be there? He always sent her out to cover the big stories and then he'd wait for her back at the office. When he wouldn't send me, I just naturally assumed he'd send her. How was I supposed to know he'd go himself?" His voice took on a note of desperation.

"Kelly, it was my only chance. If Helen was busy covering the hostage situation and another big story broke at the same time, they'd have to send me to handle it. You understand, don't you? I couldn't just sit around hoping something would break."

Kelly's blood grew colder and colder as she listened. He was a madman. And she was alone with him.

"So you just went over to Adam's house and started a fire?"

"I told you, I didn't know anyone was home. You have to believe me. I never meant to hurt anyone.

"Kelly, you can't tell anyone about this." His eyes grew wild. "You have to swear you won't say a word or I'll have to hurt you, too. And I really don't want to do that."

"We can talk about that later, Jason. Right now, we need to get you some help."

"I'm not crazy!" he practically screamed at her.

"I didn't say that. But look at you. You're very upset and…and that might trigger another attack. We don't want that to happen, now do we?" She began to maneuver around him, working her way to the door.

"Let me call the hospital or Dr. Manning. . . ." She tried to push her way past him.

"No!" He grabbed her and pulled her back into the darkroom, ripping her purse from her in the process.

She lunged again. This time he caught her and gave her a rough shove that sent her flying. She remembered grabbing at the air, groping for something to prevent her from hitting the floor. There was a sharp crack to the back of her head. Then— blackness.

21

When Kelly awoke, the acrid smell of smoke and a splitting headache drove her to her feet—and then to her knees when she tried to stand up. Her hand automatically travelled to the back of her head where the pain centered. But she pulled it away quickly when her fingers made contact with a sticky liquid oozing through her hair. She stared at her bloody hand in horror. She was in trouble—big trouble—and she knew it.

Fighting to keep her senses about her, she struggled once more to her feet, ignoring her throbbing head as best she could. She could hear the crackle now of a fire coming from behind the closed darkroom door. An orange–red haze hung in the air, plugging her nose and mouth and lungs. Her eyes stung and watered; she was coughing in uncontrolled spasms.

Kelly stumbled to the door, grabbed hold of the knob, then screamed as the searing metal burned into her flesh. The inside turnkey had partially jammed, and she knew she'd have to get a better grip on it if she was to get free.

She groped her way along the floor, feeling for a rag...a scrap of cloth...anything she could use to grip the handle, but even as she clutched at a cleaning rag under a nearby counter, unconsciousness closed in around her. She knew she didn't have much time left. Tears sprang in her eyes as desperation rose deep within her.

"You've got to calm down," she told herself outloud. "Use your head! Think!" But that was becoming more and more difficult to do as the toxic fumes from the smoke and chemicals sought to overcome her.

"Kevin knows where I am." The idea comforted her. "He's got to be worried by now. Surely he'll bring Adam." But when would they come?

"They've got to know I'm in here!" she decided. With a prayer for strength and a desperate plea for God's protection, she struggled back toward the door, screaming at the top of her lungs. Each breath shot lightning bolts of pain through her chest, but she refused to let that stop her. If Adam was out there, she would have to let him know she was alive.

22

Adam didn't stop at the drug store. . .or Maggie's. He'd finally figured it out! Kevin asked him several times what was going on, but Adam didn't answer him. He could only think of one thing—Kelly.

How could he have been so blind! The clues were all there! Jason's interest in the arson cases. . . .His immediacy on the scene at each one of them. . . .The day early date on the Freeman Factory story. . . .It all added up!

It had been Jason from the very beginning. And who knows how long he would have continued if it hadn't been for Kelly's photos?

The words of Dr. Manning echoed through his mind—"Her pupils are constricted. . . .Could be Valium but more likely it's a barbiturate of some sort."

Adam raced along the city streets, oblivious to his companions. What had happened to Kelly? Why hadn't she returned to the party? Adam had an awful feeling about the answer to that question. As he pulled into the parking lot, he saw the orange-yellow flames licking at the back of the *Bingham Daily Journal* building.

Adam slammed on the brakes, nearly sending Maggie into

the windshield in spite of her seatbelt. He threw the gearshift into park and sprang from the car. He could hear Kelly screaming as he reached the door.

"Kelly! Kelly—I'm coming!" he yelled back.

He flung open the outside doors and a blast of heat sent him reeling backward. He gulped for air, covered his head with an arm and his jacket, then dove back into the inferno. Most of the back room was ablaze and tongues of fire danced and swirled in his office. The noise surrounded him, pulsing against him.

Where was she?

He heard her scream again. The darkroom! Adam put his head down and plowed his way toward the sound. But a dozen feet from the door, something hit him from the side, sending him sprawling on the floor.

Dazed, Adam looked up into the wild eyes of Jason Roberts.

Adam froze, knowing Jason would attack again. When he lunged a second time, Adam rolled up onto his feet. He dodged Jason, then steadied himself for the next move.

He knew he was wasting time fighting Jason in the middle of this blaze. Valuable time. And Adam had become aware of an ominous silence behind the darkroom door. Every second was precious, and Adam tensed, prepared to attack. But just then, Jason went white, fell to his knees, holding his head, then convulsed in a seizure.

Adam ran to him and checked his neck for a pulse. He was alive and breathing, but with great difficulty. Adam, too, was gasping for breath as the air grew thick with the noxious gases. He was sorely tempted to leave Jason there, but knew his conscience wouldn't let him. Grabbing Jason by the legs, he dragged the lanky figure out the newsroom doors.

Kevin and Maggie were waiting outside, big question marks in their eyes.

"He's had another seizure!" Adam yelled at them. "Kelly's still inside. I'm going back for her. Stay here with Jason and call for help! Use Jason's car phone—it'll be faster!" He didn't wait for either of them to respond.

Back inside he went directly to the darkroom door. The fire had spread into the conference room and already destroyed most of the work area. Only the lobby and the darkroom remained intact.

Adam called out Kelly's name but heard no response. He tried the doorknob, but pulled away as the hot metal sent burning pain surging up his arm. He wrapped his coat around the knob, and pulled with all his might. It wouldn't budge. He dropped the coat. Stepping back, he stared at the door for an instant, then kicked with brutal force. Once, twice, three times. On the third effort, the wood cracked and splintered. The force threw him into the room.

He knelt beside the still figure. Kelly's face was ashen and lifeless. Adam's nightmare returned.

"It can't be happening again!" he cried. "Father, you can't do this to me again! Please."

Tears spilled down his cheeks. Pain enveloped him and his mind refused to function any longer. He cradled her limp body, the blood-orange smoke roiling all around.

"We have to get her out of here!" Somebody was shouting at him over the thunder of the fire and the crashing of timbers as the roof collapsed at the back of the building.

Adam looked up, but couldn't seem to focus on the face.

"Snap out of it, Wentworth! We have to go! *Now!* "

In a fog, Adam gently picked Kelly up and stumbled after the figure into the night.

The icy air hit him like a truck and made him gasp, but he managed to keep his grip on Kelly. Kevin was suddenly there beside him, throwing coats and blankets on the ground. Adam laid her body down upon them, then looked up at the surrounding faces and said simply, "She's dead."

"Get out of the way," the voice said from behind him, and Adam was pushed unceremoniously aside. It was then that he realized the voice and face belonged to George McClanahan.

The fire investigator checked for a pulse and heartbeat. When he found neither, he began cardiopulmonary resuscitation.

"How long?" he gasped between breaths and heart massage. "How long has she been unconscious?"

Adam shrugged helplessly. Time had become meaningless.

The sound of sirens wailing in the distance reached their ears. Just as the fire trucks and ambulance pulled up, Kelly gasped—and began breathing on her own again.

She coughed again, moaned, tried to roll over, then lay still. Adam rode with her to the hospital, but another night and another fire filled his mind during the trip.

Dr. Manning met them at the hospital. He rushed Kelly into emergency, stationing Adam in a connecting waiting room. Maggie and Kevin arrived shortly afterward. Together, the three of them waited in shock and silence.

Adam stared blankly at the blue cinderblock walls and the grayish-blue speckled floors. He found himself counting the number of squares in each tiled section and searching for chinks in the plastered ceiling. He picked absentmindedly at a crack in the red formaldehyde cushion of the chair he was sitting on, then pulled himself to his feet and began pacing.

He started to run his hand through his hair, but jerked it back as pain from the blisters that had formed there shook him back to reality. Maggie caught the movement. Walking over to him, she demanded that he let her examine the hand.

"You need to have this bandaged," she insisted. "This is badly blistered."

"I agree," Dr. Manning said as he came through the door and stepped beside the two of them.

"She's alive," he said to their questioning eyes, "but still unconscious."

Adam groaned.

"It's not a coma, Adam!" Dr. Manning tried to reassure him. "But it *is* serious. She's suffered a concussion, and we don't know how long she went without oxygen or what the fumes from the chemicals have done to her.

"The longer she remains unconscious, the greater the likelihood that brain damage may have occurred. We won't know anything for sure until she wakes up. The next 24 hours are critical."

Adam sank back into one of the red-cushioned chairs and buried his head in his hands, oblivious to the pain.

"What about Jason?" Maggie asked.

"He'll be all right physically," the doctor replied. "But the police have him in custody in another wing. He can't have any visitors until they're through questioning him."

"Was it the epilepsy, Doc?" Kevin asked.

The physician shook his head. "Not exactly. Not in and of itself, that is. It was Jason's reaction to the seizures that he couldn't handle. Jason's illness made him feel less of a man. And knowing that the epilepsy was the reason his mother abandoned him reinforced that poor self-image. The only thing left that provided Jason with any sort of self-worth was his work."

"If only he had known that God loves him just the way he is," Kevin said sadly. Maggie looked at Kevin, a quiet curiosity in her eyes.

Dr. Manning sent a nurse to bandage Adam's burns and wrap his hand, then allowed him to see Kelly for a few minutes. She looked frail and vulnerable, but in a strange way, peaceful, too. He drew up a chair and took her bandaged hand in his.

"What am I going to do if I lose her, Doc?" he asked.

"You're not going to lose her, Adam." Dr. Manning replied. "She isn't Helen and the situation isn't the same."

Adam stared at him, surprised.

"Kevin told me." The doctor responded to Adam's unasked question. "I am sorry about your wife, but you mustn't compare her circumstances with Kelly's. I've gotten to know Kelly pretty well over the last few months. She's a fighter—and a survivor. She's already proven that tonight. Besides, you got to Kelly right away and McClanahan was there to give her CPR. It saved her life."

"But she looks so pale. And the smoke was so terribly thick—all those poisonous gases. . .the heat. . .the flames."

"Take a good look at her, Adam," Dr. Manning ordered. Adam turned once again to caress Kelly's face with his eyes.

"There's a strength radiating from her even now." The physician noted. "She's got a powerful faith, Adam. And a powerful God."

Adam was startled at Dr. Manning's frank remark, not expecting a physician to be so candid about his faith. But the doctor went right on with his comments, oblivious to Adam's reaction.

"You know, there are fires raging around each of us every-day. And any one of them can be just as deadly as the one Kelly was in tonight. Some of them are just as visible and just as imminent. But many more are invisible and can sneak up on a person. That's the kind we have to watch out for. They smolder and suffocate their victims little by little until hope is gone and faith is dead.

"Sometimes the only way to fight fire is with fire, Adam. I believe Kelly has found the key to fighting the fires that rage around her. And that's the fire within. . . .The Spirit of God who comforts, empowers, and enables her to believe and endure.

"Now, that's not to say that Kelly's out of danger, Adam. I don't know what's in store for her. Only God Himself knows that. But whatever it is, she can handle it. . .and so can you— if you turn to the one who provides the fire of faith."

Adam thought about Dr. Manning's words through the long night. About 4:00 in the morning, Adam found himself down in the chapel. He had seemed drawn to it. . .to the place where he had released his wife and said good-bye to his daughter over a year ago.

It was deserted, now. . .the gray cushioned pews empty, a soft

177

light glowing overhead. Adam knelt before the little altar railing on the thick cushioned carpeting.

"Father," he prayed, "you said that if we confess our sins, you are faithful to forgive us, and I know that you expect the truth from us. Well, the truth is, I've never been so scared in my life. I want to believe that Kelly will survive, but I'm afraid that if I let myself hope, and you choose to take her to heaven, I won't be able to deal with it. I'm afraid I won't be able to trust you again. Maybe Doc is right, Lord. Maybe I've allowed an invisible fire to snuff out my faith. But if that's true, then what am I going to do?"

His voice broke. "Dear God, I don't have anything left to fight with. I can't do this by myself, Lord. Help me. Give me the spark, fan the flames of faith and help me fight my unbelief. Forgive me for doubting you—for denying your wisdom and sovereignty. I am your child. You are my God—just as you were Helen's and are Kelly's."

Adam felt a hand on his shoulder, and looked up into Kevin's tear-wet eyes. He knelt beside Adam and prayed, "Heavenly Father, grant Adam your gift of faith. Help him recognize the love you have for your children. Let him know your Holy Spirit is with us right now to counsel, comfort, and protect.

"As for Kelly, we know that the lives of your children are very precious to you. We know you don't take our deaths lightly. We also know you have the power to do anything, and so we ask, if it be your will, that you restore Kelly to us. Place your healing hand upon her, rekindle the spark of life within her, and give her back to us.

"But if that is not your will, Lord, then help us to remember that you have her in your arms right now. That no matter where she is—here on earth with us or with you in heaven—you are always in control. We ask for this in the name of your dear Son, Jesus Christ. Amen."

Adam felt something happen while Kevin was praying. A seed sprouted. . .a spark ignited. It wasn't very big at all, but it was enough to bring Adam a sense of peace he hadn't felt in years.

"I know it isn't easy to do," Kevin said as he and Adam rose from the altar railing, "but, remember that Kelly is in the hands of God. Don't hold her back from Him. He loves her more than anyone else could and knows exactly what to do for her. . .and for you."

Adam nodded—and knew in that instant that even though his heart was heavy over the possibility of grief, he could accept whatever happened.

23

George McClanahan was waiting for them when Adam and Kevin returned to the Intensive Care Unit. Maggie had finally been allowed to talk to Jason, the fire investigator informed them. There was still no new word on Kelly, however. Kevin went off to find Maggie, leaving Adam and George alone together.

"I don't know what to say. . . .How can I possibly thank you for saving Kelly's life?" Adam finally broke the silence. "I guess that perhaps I should start by apologizing. I was wrong about you, George. I know now you did everything possible to catch the arsonist. I'm sorry I said those things. You're a good man, and I'll say that publicly in the very next issue of the *Journal*."

The fire investigator's face reddened at the unexpected announcement. "Well, now. You don't have to do anything like that. Truth is, I was mighty unfair to you, too. . .jumping on you the way I did and accusing you of being involved with all of this. Yesterday I found a gold pinkie ring in the old apartment complex. Guess we know now that it was Jason's–as if we needed anymore proof. As for Miss Jordan. . .I was just doing my duty. I would have done the same for anyone."

were just rounding a corner of the building as he paid the taxi driver.

Adam stiffened at the sight of them.

"I guess you probably know the whole story by now," he said as he walked over to them.

"Yes," Vincent spoke for them both. "McClanahan filled us in on most of it." Rosselli's tone held a note of suspicion. "How's Kelly doing?"

"According to Dr. Manning, she should recover—physically, that is. I'm not so sure how any of us is going to recover from this emotionally, though.

"It's going to be tough for all of us, I know. But I can start to settle some things right now by telling you both how sorry I am for accusing you the way I did at the party last night."

He turned to Whitney. "I deeply regret all the animosity that's existed between us lately. I wish things could have worked out differently. And I know that Kelly feels the same way about you, too, Vince. I know there isn't much chance of us ever being friends, but I hope we can stop clawing at each other's throats." Adam extended his bandaged hand, but neither of them would take it.

Adam shook his head sadly and sighed. "Have it your way, then." He turned and left them standing there.

Adam didn't bother to shower or change when he got home; he just collapsed with exhaustion onto his bed. It was late afternoon before he finally awoke. His hand was throbbing and he was so stiff and sore, he could hardly move.

A long steaming shower partially revived him, and he grabbed a quick cup of coffee before he left for the hospital.

When he arrived, Kelly's family had just left, he was informed at the desk, and she had just been moved out of Intensive Care. He rapped lightly on her door, then entered without waiting for an answer.

"How are you doing?" he asked.

She turned toward him and smiled her answer back at him.

He went to her and sat at the edge of her bed, gathering her in his arms.

"Thank God. Thank God you're all right," he cried softly. "Don't you ever—ever—do that to me again."

Kelly whispered hoarsely that she didn't have any plans to repeat the performance.

"Plans?" Dr. Manning entered the room. "What's this I hear about plans? You two setting a wedding date?"

"That's a rather presumptuous question, Doctor," Adam replied, his face flushing.

"I don't think so," the physician declared, his eyes crinkling in amusement. "It seems to me you're the only two people here, who haven't figured out you belong together."

Kelly spent the next ten days in the hospital. Adam spent every single one of them with her and enjoyed meeting her family.

The doctors kept a close watch on her condition, concerned about the possibility of pneumonia. But there were only good reports.

The news about the *Bingham Daily Journal* was not so encouraging. The place had been totaled and corporate executives weren't sure they wanted to rebuild. They offered Adam a position at one of their other papers in another town, as well as offering to retrain and/or relocate the remaining staff.

"I know it may be a mistake to leave the security of a big corporation," he told Kelly when he related the offer he'd received, "but I'm not sure I want to work for someone else again. It's been kind of a secret dream of mine to run my own publication someday. Maybe this is the time to do it. I've saved enough for a substantial down payment on a small paper or magazine, and I'm sure I could borrow the rest. It's a big step, but if I don't do it now, maybe I never will."

Kelly fell silent as she thought about what he was saying. He seemed so sure of himself. And she didn't know where she was

186

going or what she'd be doing in the next few months. The only thing she did know was that she wanted Adam Wentworth to be a part of her future. The only problem was that Adam hadn't indicated he felt the same way. She finally responded with, "If that's what you believe God is leading you to do—then go for it. I know you'll do great."

But all during her recovery, Adam never said a word about the two of them working together. It was always what "he" wanted or what "he" hoped to do. Never "we." And as the date of her discharge from the hospital grew nearer, so did her anxiety.

It was cold and gray the day she was released from the Medical Center. Delays in the paperwork kept her from leaving until late in the afternoon. In fact, darkness had already crept in on the town when Adam finally brought his car around for her.

He was unusually subdued and didn't say much as he drove her home. When they got to her apartment, Adam turned off the engine but made no move to get out. When she reached for her door handle, he laid a restraining hand on her arm.

"Kelly, wait. I've got something to tell you." His eyes met hers. "I'm going to be leaving Bingham soon."

Icy fingers of dread crawled up her spine. She hadn't even considered the possibility that he would leave town now that he'd turned down the corporation's offer. But then she realized how short-sighted that had been on her part. Of course, he'd have to go wherever the new offices were.

She wanted to tell him not to go. . .that she couldn't bear to live her life without him. . .but she knew she couldn't stand in the way of his dream.

"I see." She wasn't sure what else she should say. "When?"

"Next week. I'm going to check out a newspaper that's for sale in Colorado. If I like it, I'll move out there permanently."

Kelly turned away from him and stared out the window, trying to hide the tears that insisted upon sneaking down her cheeks. It had begun to snow. Powdered-sugar snow, fine and steady. The icy winter air stole into the car and settled in her heart, chilling her to the bone. She shivered.

Adam got out of the car and came around to her side. He opened the door and held out his hand for her, but she waved him away.

As she stepped out onto the snow-covered pavement, however, her foot slid out from under her. Adam grabbed hold of her and brought her firmly to both feet. She leaned back against the car, his hands steadying her under each elbow, trapping her there with his gaze.

His wet, curly hair sparkled like diamond dust under the street lamp. His silver eyes were sharp and clear and seemed to see all the way into her soul.

Kelly forgot to breathe for a moment; his nearness wiped out everything in her mind except the pain of the loss she was about to know.

He lightly brushed some snow out of her hair, then caressed her cheek with his gloved hand. There was such sadness in her heart, Kelly could hardly stand it.

How can I let him walk away? she cried to herself. *How can I survive without him?* Tears choked in her throat. Adam remained still, staring at her, turmoil boiling in his eyes.

"I can't do this!" he suddenly said. "I can't leave the way things are now." He took a sharp breath. "Kelly, I know I have no right to ask you this. Not with my future so uncertain, but I simply can't wait until I get back from Colorado. I have to know now, before I leave. . . .

"Kelly?" he said sharply, then softened his tone. "Kelly, would you marry me?. . ." He went on quickly before she could answer.

"I know I have nothing to offer you. I can't even promise I'll be able to support you. . ."

"Yes," she interrupted him.

"I know that buying a newspaper is a risky business and if I fail, we'll be bankrupt, but I don't even want to try if you're not going to be with me. . . ."

"Adam. . ." she broke in again.

". . .Don't say 'no' right away. Just think about it, okay?"

"Adam!"

"What?" He finally stopped to catch his breath.

Kelly gave a long dramatic pause then repeated her answer. "I said, 'yes,' I'll marry you." She beamed up at him.

Adam broke into a wide grin and, for the first time in a long time, laughed right out loud.

He grabbed her around the waist and whirled around, sending the powdered snow flying. When Kelly was back on the ground, she flashed him a smile that lit up the whole parking lot. And Kelly saw fire dancing in his eyes.